Saunders
Physical
Activities
Series

Edited by

MARYHELEN VANNIER, Ed.D.

Professor and Director, Women's Division,
Department of Health and Physical Education,
Southern Methodist University

HOLLIS F. FAIT, Ph.D.

Professor of Physical Education,
School of Physical Education,
University of Connecticut

THIRD EDITION

POWER VOLLEYBALL

Thomas Slaymaker, Ed.D.

International Referee
Formerly Assistant Professor of Physical Education
Central Missouri State College
Warrensburg, Missouri

Virginia H. Brown, B.S., M.S.

Shawnee Mission Kansas School District

Illustrated by Vernon Hüppi

 SAUNDERS COLLEGE PUBLISHING

Philadelphia   New York   Chicago
San Francisco   Montreal   Toronto
London   Sydney   Tokyo   Mexico City
Rio de Janeiro   Madrid

821827

Address orders to:
383 Madison Avenue
New York, NY 10017

Address editorial correspondence to:
West Washington Square
Philadelphia, PA 19105

Text Typeface: 10/12 Press Roman
Compositor: TechType Graphics
Acquisitions Editor: John Butler
Project Editor: Don Reisman
Copyeditor: Lauren Cusick
Managing Editor and Art Director: Richard L. Moore
Design Assistant: Virginia A. Bollard
Text Design: Phoenix Studio, Inc.
Cover Design: Richard L. Moore
Production Manager: Tim Frelick
Assistant Production Manager: Maureen Read

Cover credit: Artwork drawn by Tom Mallon.

POWER VOLLEYBALL

ISBN 0-03-062837-7

2345 090 987654321

CBS COLLEGE PUBLISHING
Saunders College Publishing
Holt, Rinehart and Winston
The Dryden Press

EDITORS' FOREWORD

Every period of history, as well as every society, has its own profile. Our own world of the last third of the twentieth century is no different. Whenever we step back to look at ourselves, we can see excellences and failings, strengths and weaknesses, that are peculiarly ours.

One of our strengths as a nation is that we are a sports-loving people. Today more persons — and not just young people — are playing, watching, listening to, and reading about sports and games. Those who enjoy themselves most are the men and women who actually *play* the game: the "doers."

You are reading this book now for either of two very good reasons. First, you want to learn — whether in a class or on your own — how to play a sport well, and you need clear, easy-to-follow instructions to develop the special skills involved. If you want to be a successful player, this book will be of much help to you.

Second, you may already have developed skill in this activity, but want to improve your performance through assessing your weaknesses and correcting your errors. You want to develop further the skills you have now and to learn and perfect additional ones. You realize that you will enjoy the activity even more if you know more about it.

In either case, this book can contribute greatly to your success. It offers "lessons" from a real professional: from an outstandingly successful coach, teacher, or performer. All the authors in the *Saunders Physical Activities Series* are experts and widely recognized in their specialized fields. Some have been members or coaches of teams of national prominence and Olympic fame.

This book, like the others in our Series, has been written to make it easy for you to help yourself to learn. The author and the editors want you to become more self-motivated and to gain a greater understanding of, appreciation for, and proficiency in the exciting world of *movement*. All the activities described in this Series — sports, games, dance, body conditioning, and weight and figure control activities — require skillful, efficient movement. That's what physical activity is all about. Each book contains descriptions and helpful tips about the nature, value, and purpose of an activity, about the purchase and care of equipment, and about the fundamentals of each movement skill involved. These books also tell you about common errors and how to avoid making them, about ways in which you can improve your performance, and about game rules and strategy, scoring, and special techniques. Above all, they should tell you how to get the most pleasure and benefit from the time you spend.

Our purpose is to make you a successful *participant* in this age of sports activities. If you are successful, you will participate often — and this will give you countless hours of creative and recreative fun. At the same time, you will become more physically fit.

"Physical fitness" is more than just a passing fad or a slogan. It is a condition of your body which determines how effectively you can perform your daily work and play and how well you can meet unexpected demands on your strength, your physical skills, and your endurance. How fit you are depends largely on your participation in vigorous physical activity. Of course no one sports activity can provide the kind of total workout of the body required to achieve optimal fitness; but participation with vigor in any activity makes a significant contribution to this total. Consequently, the activity you will learn through reading this book can be extremely helpful to you in developing and maintaining physical fitness now and throughout the years to come.

These physiological benefits of physical activity are important beyond question. Still, the pure pleasure of participation in physical activity will probably provide your strongest motivation. The activities taught in this Series are *fun,* and they provide a most satisfying kind of recreation for your leisure hours. Also they offer you great personal satisfaction in achieving success in skillful performance — in the realization that you are able to control your body and its movement and to develop its power and beauty. Further, there can be a real sense of fulfillment in besting a skilled opponent or in exceeding a goal you have set for yourself. Even when you fall short of such triumphs, you can still find satisfaction in the effort you have made to meet a challenge. By participating in sports you can gain greater respect for yourself, for others, and for "the rules of the game." Your skills in leadership and fellowship will be sharpened and improved. Last, but hardly least, you will make new friends among others who enjoy sports activities, both as participants and as spectators.

We know you're going to enjoy this book. We hope that it — and the others in our Series — will make you a more skillful and more enthusiastic performer in all the activities you undertake.

Good luck!

MARYHELEN VANNIER
HOLLIS FAIT

PREFACE

Power Volleyball has been written for college and secondary level participants in a rapidly developing sport. The information contained in this book is intended to be used by both female and male participants at these levels. Many knowledgeable people concerned with the development of the sport for both sexes have become increasingly aware that the skills and strategy involved are very similar for both men and women. Generally speaking, what the female players lack in all-out power and strength, they make up in agility and flexibility. The similarity in the games played by the two sexes is recognized by The United States Volleyball Association, the governing body for the sport in this country. In their rules guide the sole disparity in rules for men and women lies in the height of the net. There is, however, a slight difference between the U.S.V.B. A. rules and the rules for women published by the Division for Girls' and Women's Sports (D.G.W.S.). The differences have become less and less distinct in the past few years, to the point that teams playing under different rules are able to reconcile those differences with only a slight adjustment in strategy and technique. For this reason, we have made no attempt in this book to discuss the minor differences that do exist between the U.S.V.B.A. and the D.G.W.S.

While it is true that the basic purpose of this book is to increase the enjoyment in participation for the player, the authors also hope that the sections of the book devoted to rules and strategy, advanced skills, and practice hints will be of considerable help to the teacher or coach in the sport.

THOMAS SLAYMAKER

VIRGINIA H. BROWN

CONTENTS

1☐Emphasis, Values, and Significant History

The game of volleyball has become recognized as one of the leading participation sports in the world. While the exact number of people actually playing the game each year is impossible to determine, estimates range from 50 to 80 million participants throughout the world. The game has been found to be the leading competitive sport in at least 25 different countries. When volleyball was finally admitted to the official list of sports in the Olympic Games in 1964, the game achieved the recognition it deserved. For many years before that, however, volleyball had an international flavor with teams representing their respective countries in the Pan American Games, the European Championships, the Asiatic Championships, and the World Games. It has not been uncommon for two teams meeting for the European Championships to play before 40,000 spectators.

In the United States, the growth of volleyball has followed a somewhat different pattern. The game itself has an American origin, having been invented in 1895 by William G. Morgan, physical director of the Holyoke, Massachusetts, YMCA. Changes in technical rules and in equipment occurred fairly rapidly, but the development of the game into a highly competitive sport was a lengthy process.

The leading organizational group in the development of good tournament volleyball has been, and is presently, the United States Volleyball Association (USVBA), formed in 1928. The USVBA itself is made up of 22 different organizations, such as the American Alliance for Health, Physical Education and Recreation; the National Council of YMCAs; and the Amateur Athletic Union. Each year the association organizes a national tournament for the collegiate division, the women's open division, the YMCA division, the senior men's division, and the men's open division. Usually 1000 or more athletes gather to participate in these championships. Despite publicity efforts on the part of the news media and the host association, it is not uncommon at these matches for the officials and the players whose teams have been eliminated from the tournament to outnumber other spectators.

1

Interest in volleyball as a participant sport and possibly as a spectator sport is increasing. Probably the reason for this increased interest lies in the fact that more and more young athletes are discovering that volleyball properly played has much to offer in the way of competition, conditioning, relaxation and joy of participation. A few states are encouraging competition for boys and girls at the state championship level, and many states encourage interschool competition at lower than state tournament levels. Many colleges are beginning to field varsity teams for both men and women. Players for these school teams are often selected from student populations that have had experience in the game of power volleyball at the intramural level. Having played the game as it should be played, many of these participants will continue to participate in recreation and church leagues and a few will advance to the highly skilled type of play offered for both men and women at the YMCA's and open tournaments. Others, while not actually participating in power volleyball, will support the game as spectators, perhaps becoming a part of future Olympic Game sellout crowds, such as were frequently seen at Mexico City in 1968 and Munich in 1972.

POWER VOLLEYBALL

The term "power volleyball" has been coined in recent years to describe a type of volleyball played at a more highly competitive level than the usual recreational game. The term is well chosen, since one of the more dramatic plays in the game at the advanced level is the well executed spike, which has been timed at speeds ranging from 60 to 90 miles an hour! Speed, power, and mastery of skills characterize the game. While the basic rules of the contest are very similar to recreational volleyball, there are many refinements that create a dramatically new type of activity. The degree of ability in the many skills necessary and the understanding of strategy by participants will determine the degree of competition between any two teams. However, any group may attempt to play power volleyball if it has a simple understanding of techniques and rule interpretations.

How Power Volleyball is Played

As in recreational volleyball, each point begins when the ball is served from behind the base line on the right side of the court. In power volleyball, this serve is usually a forcefully hit, overhead type of floater serve. The action of the ball in its flight when served in this manner makes it difficult for the receiving team to field the ball effectively. There is a drastic difference between the type of individual effort used to receive the serve in power volleyball and the type of reception used in the recreational game. The receiving player in power volleyball must play the ball cleanly without letting the ball visibly come to rest or without making double contact with the ball. In recent years, nearly all participants in the game of power volleyball have resorted to an underhand "bump" pass to receive the serve. If the reception of the serve is successfully controlled, the ball will travel from the receiver to the player occupying a position in the front line, normally called the setter.

There are many offensive maneuvers that may be employed once the ball has traveled to the setter, but basically, each maneuver depends on the ability of the setter to place the ball in a desired position above and several feet back from the net. One of three legal spikers then approaches the net, times his vertical jump to the descent of the ball, and attempts to spike the ball forcefully into the opponents' court. The serving team becomes the defensive team immediately after the serve and should prepare to meet the offensive thrust or spike of the opponents by a series of defensive maneuvers. If the ball has been skillfully served, the serve reception may be faulty and result in the set man of the offense being deprived of the ball. In the latter case, players move to predetermined positions to cover the court on the return. In the play situation already described, however, where the ball has been well placed by the setter, the defensive team will attempt to have two (sometimes three) of its front line players jump high in the air at a position at the net directly opposite the ball, to block it. During this action, the offensive spiker is attempting to employ some type of offensive tactic that will "put the ball away" on the opposite side of the net. The spiker may attempt to hit the ball over or around the block on a hard-driven spike, or he may simply "dink" the ball (a soft lob) to an uncovered area of the opponents' court. The defensive team must endeavor to cover as much of its court as possible, utilizing the three or four players not taking part in the block.

If the spiker is able to overcome the block and the ball is not returned, the spiker's team gains the serve and the opportunity to score points. If the blocking team prevails and the ball is "stuffed" back onto the floor of the spiking team, the serving team has scored a point and wins the right to serve again. Frequently, however, the spiked ball hits the block and continues in play on one side of the court. If the ball is blocked back into the spiker's court, the players on the team will simply treat the situation as the start of a new play and will attempt to play the ball to the set man in the front line who, in turn, will set his spikers. If the ball rebounds from the block and continues into the court on the blocker's side of the net, the team still has three hits remaining to place its offense into effect because current rules do not count the block as one of the three hits allowed each team. The opposing team has its block deployed and attempts to defend against this new offensive thrust.

Play continues, of course, until one team is unable to return the ball in its allowed three hits or until a foul is committed. Variations in offensive and defensive strategy are numerous, and the participants must learn to recognize the rapid change from offense to defense and react accordingly. The basic techniques in volleyball remain the same, however; and players must become proficient in all skills, including the serve, the bump pass, the set, the spike, and the block, for successful participation in power volleyball.

VALUES

While enjoyment in playing a game of power volleyball is readily recognized by the player as a value of participation, there are other benefits that are less easily identified. These values may be grouped generally into four categories of personal growth and development: physical, motor, psychological, and sociological.

Physical Growth

Any individual taking part in a vigorous schedule of training and practice for a competitive activity such as power volleyball may expect improvement in several basic facets of physical fitness: strength, endurance, speed, balance, and flexibility. Strength plays a major role in the vertical jumping ability necessary in the basic spike and block for all players. Most conditioning programs for power volleyball stress a need to improve leg strength in an effort to increase vertical jumping ability. Endurance gains are brought about by the necessity for an individual player to be constantly on the move in a well played game of power volleyball. It is true that a player is seldom required to run more than 15 or 20 feet, but it is also true that a minimum amount of time is spent in simply standing still. Speed, in the sense of movement of body segments, is also improved in the participant in the modern game. The ability to recognize the direction a ball is going to be spiked, a quick total body movement in that direction, and a very rapid thrust of the hand to intercept the ball, traveling at speeds of about 60 miles an hour, demand a high degree of speed of movement.

Another aspect of physical development is that of improved balance. Not only must a player be able to display a degree of static balance in several of the skill "ready" positions, but dynamic balance must also be demonstrated. Balance must be in evidence, particularly at the net, where a spiker is expected to approach the net, jump high in the air, spike a ball with considerable power, and then land and regain his balance almost instantly in order to take part in any ensuing action. A very important physical aspect of today's game of volleyball is flexibility. Players preparing to participate in power volleyball must be certain that improved flexibility is a factor in any workout plan. In women's competition, in particular, a great deal of player effort is directed toward stretching and reaching for the ball. The Japanese women in the last two Olympic Game competitions have demonstrated an amazing amount of flexibility in their total play patterns.

Motor Development

Overall body coordination is developed as a result of the necessity for the participant in power volleyball to become a master of many different skills. Players cannot hope to succeed in the game if only one specialty, such as serving or blocking, is well developed at the expense of total skill development. While there is some degree of carry-over benefit from (and into) different games, volleyball skills are almost unique. For example, it is obvious that a player with an unusually high vertical jump may have an advantage over players with less jumping ability, but jumping ability will be an advantage only when proper arm action, eye–hand coordination, and timing are developed into an overall spiking skill.

A phase of motor development that is not generally recognized as part of the development resulting from volleyball is agility. Since the ball is constantly in motion and the court is occupied by five other players moving to different court positions as the team goes from offense to defense, the player must learn body control in response to the ever-changing situation. The high agility level of a skilled player is readily demonstrated as he or she takes a few quick steps, dives headlong for an errant ball, returns the ball high into the air, executes a shoulder roll upon contact with the floor, and immediately gets up.

Psychological Development

There are several values of a psychological nature to be obtained from power volleyball. The player must learn self-discipline in order that the playing rights of others are not violated. It takes a high degree of self-discipline for a skilled player to "stay at home" and watch a player with less ability attempt a play that might be completed if he or she were to be a "ball hog." At the same time, all players learn a high degree of personal responsibility toward their teammates when making plays that come into their area. Personal integrity and regard for rules are traits that are strengthened as players learn to accept the judgment of the first and second referees and the linesmen assigned to officiate the contest without showing displeasure or disgust as ball handling violations or net touches are called on individual players.

A slightly different aspect of psychological benefit might be included when one considers the mental outlook of an individual before and after a vigorous workout. It is extremely difficult to carry the problems of everyday existence into an active session of vigorous activity such as power volleyball. Many busy students and adults find mental refreshment in an hour's participation in power volleyball in the middle of the day.

Sociological Growth

Several sociological considerations might be made regarding power volleyball. Recreation experts are very vocal in expressing the view that we all must increase our ability to utilize constructively our increasing leisure time. Volleyball is an excellent activity for both sexes. It requires a minimum of equipment and play space and provides maximum opportunity for co-ed participation as well as separate contests for men and women. Volleyball also promotes increased socialization by teammates both on and off the court. Many participants in the game acknowledge that the time spent in socializing after a contest is as important as the time spent in play. Many lasting friendships have been made during tournament play when players not actually engaged in a contest gather to exchange ideas and pleasantries with players from other areas. Co-ed volleyball lends itself especially well to this type of social activity!

FUTURE EMPHASIS

Despite the apparent increase in numbers of participants and the slight increase in spectator interest, many individuals familiar with the sport are concerned with the eventual place of volleyball in our sports-oriented society. There are too many young people of junior and senior high-school age as well as many college students who never experience a power volleyball contest, either as a player or as a spectator. Younger participants in the sport should be encouraged to increase the skills necessary for enjoyable competition. High school and college students should be allowed to progress toward participation in advanced stages of competition. Young adults participating in leagues or recreational volleyball should encourage others to adhere to the regulations and style of play necessary for power volleyball. Experienced players of any age should make themselves available for clinics, teaching demonstrations, and exhibitions, as well as serving as officials for sports days, interschool competition, and the like. Finally, as more and more men and women experience the benefits and enjoyment of participation in power volleyball, overall support of the activity will continue to grow, until the sport of volleyball is recognized by all to be a valuable part of our total school and recreational scene.

2 □ Playing Area and Equipment

SAFETY CONSIDERATIONS

Before entering into a discussion and description of actual court dimensions and equipment, it is necessary to consider the volleyball playing area in the light of player safety. As players gain skill in the various aspects of volleyball, enthusiasm and an increase in player mobility or range of movement result. Players should be well aware of any and all possible obstructions that might present a safety hazard to participants. The following court conditions might well be taken into consideration and attempts made at correction before play begins.

Movable Objects

Often one of the most serious safety hazards facing a group of volleyball participants is the failure to remove miscellaneous objects from the playing surface outside the court boundaries. Many objects used in normal physical education classes constitute a real danger when not removed from the volleyball court area. Such items as parallel bars, vaulting horses, tables and chairs, mats, and the like should be removed as far as possible, if not altogether, from the court or courts. If heavy pieces of equipment, such as portable basketball goals or balance beams, cannot be completely removed, they should be placed as far from the court as possible and positioned to present a minimum of sharp corners.

Close Walls

In many existing facilities, when one or more courts are set up, the court boundary lines are very close to side walls or rear walls. As there is usually little or nothing that can be done to alleviate this problem, the danger must be recognized by the players before they begin to play. They should also note any unusual and hazardous features on the wall surfaces, such as drinking fountains, chalk rails, or folded bleachers.

Multiple Courts

When two or more courts are laid out in a gymnasium that is large enough to accommodate more than one court, usually only a short distance separates one court from another. Under these circumstances, players should exercise caution in pursuing an errant ball, that is still in play, into an adjacent court; they should make the players of that court aware of the presence of the ball so that play may be suspended momentarily. It is very important that players recognize the necessity for halting play so that a stray ball can be removed; otherwise serious injury may result from a player landing on a ball and being thrown badly off balance. Play interrupted for a "ball on the court" should be replayed with no point or sideout being counted.

Floor Condition

Players should be aware that the condition of the floor is instrumental in assuring safe playing conditions. Normal maintenance and cleaning are certainly sufficient to ensure a safe floor surface for class or tournament volleyball. Undusted floors or floors with an accumulation of waste materials, such as gum wrappers or bobby pins, present a slick surface that is hardly conducive to the fast movement and rapid change of direction that takes place in power volleyball. Occasionally a player attempting to retrieve a ball in a diving save leaves an area of the floor damp with perspiration, creating a real hazard. When this occurs, time out should be called and the floor wiped dry.

Net Supports

Because of the degree of net tension desirable in a good court set-up, it is frequently necessary to attach the net to permanent fixtures by means of guy wires or ropes. Players should note the attachment of these wires or ropes and the presence of a permanent referee's stand in order that they may be avoided during play. When it is necessary to attach tension wires to the floor, such lines must be noted before play begins and well marked with strips of rag or tape to make them clearly visible to both players and spectators.

COURT DIMENSIONS

The regulation six-man team volleyball court shown in Figure 2–1 has outside dimensions of 18 meters by 9 meters. In some gymnasiums, additional

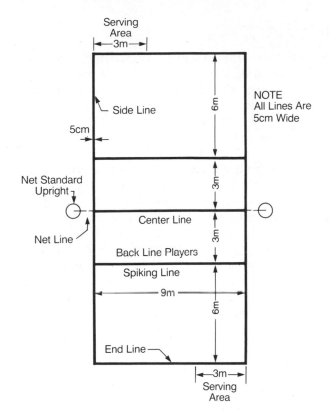

Figure 2-1. Dimensions of volleyball court.

courts can be obtained by simply reducing one or both distances. Although this shrinking of the playing surface is hardly desirable, the sacrifice would seem advisable in order to increase the total number of participants.

In addition to side and rear boundary lines, a center line and two back court attack lines, each 3 meters from the center line and parallel to it, are necessary for complete court markings. The two lines marking the serving zone for both men's and women's courts are placed 3 meters from the right side line. All lines on a regulation court are 2 inches (5 cm) wide. While the current court dimensions are given in meters, it must be acknowledged that many existing facilities currently have courts marked in feet (60 by 30 with 10-foot back court attack lines). Since only a 6-inch reduction in size results in the overall court dimension of a metric court, courts marked in the old dimensions may be used with virtually no noticeable difference in overall play. Temporary court boundary lines may be improvised with pressure-sensitive tape that can be easily removed if necessary.

Ceiling and Side Zones

In addition to the court surface itself, consideration should be given to ceiling height and distances from side and rear boundary lines to walls or nets hung between courts to restrict wildly hit balls. A minimum ceiling height of 26 feet is necessary for tournament volleyball, and a minimum height of 22 feet seems necessary for most play situations. When volleyball is played with lower ceilings or where obstructions hanging from the ceiling impede play, it will probably be necessary to create ground rules dealing with play situations in which the normal path of the ball is interrupted. The usual ruling in these instances is to allow a team member to play the ball off the obstruction or ceiling provided it remains on his side of the net and provided the team has not utilized its three hits.

Side and rear areas adjacent to boundary lines are usually predetermined by the total space available, but if courts are to be placed with these zones taken into consideration, a minimum of 10 feet in the side zones and 15 feet in the rear-court zones is desirable. These distances do not include seating areas for substitutes or spectators. In playing sites that include spectator space on the general floor surface, extreme care should be given to maintaining the whole floor and not just the actual playing court.

The Net and Net Standards

Probably the second most important aspect of ensuring an enthusiastic volleyball program (next to excellent instruction and supervision) is a properly rigged net. While the height of the net is certainly important, other factors contribute to ideal net conditions. The top of the net should be strung with a $3/8$-inch steel cable with loops at both ends, and the bottom of the net should be threaded with (or taped to) a $3/8$-inch hemp rope with 15 feet of excess at both ends of the net. Figure 2–2 shows the structure of a typical tournament net and referee stand.

A desirable and frequently used standard for routine class play is an automobile tire and wheel filled with cement and attached to a 2 inch pipe. The pipe should have strong eye bolts at heights of 7 feet, 7 feet 6 inches, and 8 feet 12 inches. The eye bolts should have an opening at the top sufficiently wide to allow the steel net cable to be attached by the end loops. The rope in the bottom of the net may be tied to the standards with sufficient pull to provide good net tension.

The standards should be secured to permanent wall or floor fixtures in such a manner as to allow tension adjustment. Ingenuity is more important in this operation than extensive or expensive and elaborate equipment. Thoughtful use of rope, additional steel cable, turnbuckles, or existing floor plates and wall fixtures generally ensures acceptable net height and tautness for all types of play.

The height from the floor to the top of the net will vary with the type of player using the facility. Accomplished male participants play with a net height of 2.43 meters (7 feet 11⅝ inches) whereas accomplished women players use a

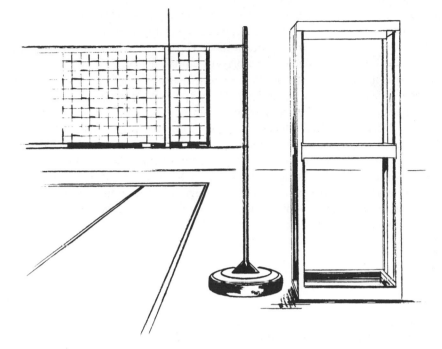

Figure 2-2. Typical net structure and referee's stand.

2.29 meter (7 foot 4¹/₈ inch) net. Inexperienced players of both sexes may desire an opportunity to experience success in net play by using a net at a height somewhat less than what is official for their sex. Inexperienced men might utilize a 7-foot 6-inch net while women might have a 7-foot net. Younger players of shorter than average height should be allowed to play over a net approximately 1 foot over the raised hand of a child of average height. Emphasis is placed on the fact that the average height player, disregarding age or class level, should be able to achieve success at the net with some degree of regularity even if it means lowering the net to heights lower than those already mentioned. A final net consideration is the use of tape or other material to designate the vertical boundary of the net. This tape should be 2 inches wide and placed from the top to the bottom of the net directly over each side line. In tournament play, current rules provide that vertical antennae be placed on the outer edge of the vertical boundary tape on each side of the net. These antennae should extend 2¹/₂ to 3¹/₂ feet above the top of the net and are specifically utilized to denote the legality of a ball being returned across the net. (See Fig. 2-2)

Referee's Stand — Scoreboards

Participants in the game concerned with volleyball courts that are to be used for interschool matches or extensive intramural play may equip the court with a referee's stand and a scoreboard for each court. A temporary stand may be erected by utilizing a medium size stepladder or sturdy table at one end of the net no less than 3 feet from the side line. The 3-foot minimum distance is a necessity to lessen the chance of a player's contacting the referee's stand. If a more permanent referee's stand is desired, a platform may be constructed to include uprights of sufficient bracing to allow upper net attachment to them.

Permanent or specially built referee's stands can usually be constructed so as to allow placement of a mechanical scoreboard for each team on the stand. Such scoreboards are helpful to beginning classes and are a must for advanced play. If no permanent electric or mechanical score keeping devices are available, inexpensive boards may be constructed. Use a 2-foot square of ³/₄-inch plywood painted white with black numbers (1 through 15) and a simply made metal arrow attached to the middle of the square in such a manner that it may be rotated to indicate the correct score.

VOLLEYBALLS

A standard volleyball has a circumference of 25 to 27 inches and weighs 9 to 10 ounces. In the United States, the ball is usually white although some imported balls are light tan or yellow. Inflation pressure is always stated on the ball and should be strictly adhered to in order to assure normal feel and ball life expectancy. Players should become familiar with the feel of a properly inflated ball and should strive to maintain the correct pressure of the ball.

Careful consideration should be given to the type of usage expected for the ball when determining the type of ball to be purchased. The fact that a rubber ball will outlast even the toughest leather ball should be considered in light of the loss of feel that is experienced when using a rubber ball. Several reliable manufacturers (some domestic, some Japanese) are now producing a relatively inexpensive leather ball that has shown an amazing durability. Since this "new" type of volleyball has consistently held its shape and size during extensive use, it is now used almost universally in tournament play and intercollegiate competition as well as in many YMCAs, YWCAs, high schools, and colleges during practice.

Whatever ball is purchased, normal care and periodic cleaning will result in longer ball life as well as a better feel during play or practice. Since all volleyballs are subject to puncture or become misshapen when abused, volleyballs should never be kicked or constantly hit into rough or abrasive surfaces. Overinflation is very abusive to a volleyball.

3 □ Conditioning

Before entering into a discussion of the basic skills for both male and female participants in power volleyball, it is necessary to examine the general overall physical aspects of successful players at several levels of competition. There is little doubt that the players representing their respective countries in such international competition as the Olympic Games or the Pan American Games are superbly conditioned, well trained men and women. These players combine excellent physical prowess with advanced team and individual knowledge and strategy to produce the ultimate in competition in this modern day game of power volleyball. Men and women competing at the regional level in USVBA-sanctioned tournaments display many of the same individual skills and much the same team strategy as those used by the more advanced teams. The physical abilities and conditioning of these competitors are generally superior to those of the general public. Finally, young men and women participating at the college or secondary level soon learn that before many basic skills can be improved or mastered, an overall improvement of certain aspects of basic fitness must be accomplished. This chapter will examine certain general areas of overall motor fitness in relation to the manner in which these areas effect mastery of volleyball skills.

THE LEGS

One of the most dramatic revelations in examining the physical differences in the players competing in international matches lies in the extreme variation in vertical jumping ability of the men from various countries. In a recent tour through Canada, the Russian team had a team-average vertical jump that was greater than the greatest height attained by a United States representative. At lesser levels of competition, one has but to observe teams in action to realize that one of the most basic movements in volleyball for the individual player is the vertical jump. The jumping action is used in almost all plays at the net, and the successful completion of a spike or block often depends entirely on the ability of the player to leap to a position of advantage above the net before bringing skills into use.

Improving Leg Power

To achieve maximum jumping potential, players must be willing to devote a certain period (15 to 25 minutes) each day to specific activities directed at improving leg power. Most of the training exercises specified will have the added effect of improving overall endurance, as cardiovascular improvements occur naturally, as well as improvement in muscular strength. In many cases, it will be necessary to begin with fewer repetitions or less time spent on each drill until strength and endurance are improved.

Leg squats with weights

Increase the speed with which improvement takes place by gradually increasing the amount of weight used from one third of your total body weight to one half (or perhaps 60 percent in some instances) of your total body weight. Place the weight selected on your shoulders and spread the feet apart to shoulder width. Stand flat footed and keep the trunk in an upright posture. Squat to a level beteween quarter squats and half squats and return to a standing position. Do 10 to 15 repetitions before pausing and attempt to complete three sets in each workout. If initial weight does not seem to bring about exertion during the last of three sets, more weight should be added in subsequent workouts.

Toe raises with weights

Select a weight to be placed on the shoulders by using the same basic formula used in weight selection for leg squats (one third to one half the body weight). Stand with the toes and balls of the feet on a solid surface 2 to 3 inches above floor level. (A 2-inch board is generally satisfactory.) Using the muscles of the legs only, raise to a full extension position with the heels as far from the floor as possible. Then lower the heels slowly until they make contact with the floor. The legs should control the rate of descent of body and added weight, so that the body does not simply drop from the full extension position. Repeat the raising and lowering of the body 15 to 20 times, doing the exercise fairly rapidly. Try to complete three sets during each workout.

Jumping for height

You should include two types of jumps during each workout session, or possibly alternate days and do a full number of repetitions for each type of jump. In each case, an object suspended at a height of 9 to 12 feet, depending on basic reach and jumping ability, is necessary. (A basketball net, goal, or backboards usually are ideal for this purpose.) In the standing jump, stand under the target and without taking an approach step, jump and reach as high as possible three times in rapid succession. Rest 10 seconds and repeat the three jumps. Alternate the arm action during each set of three jumps by alternating a full reach with both arms (as in a block in volleyball) and a fully extended striking action at the top of the jump (as in a volleyball spike). Start with 10 sets of three jumps (30 total) and strive to reach a 25-set maximum (75 total jumps).

The second jumping method to be used is a two- or three-step approach to a point directly under the target followed by a full jump utilizing either of the arm actions previously described. In both methods, be sure to utilize the mechanics of good jumping, including an almost full squat and a violent upward thrusting of the arm as you leave the ground.

Rope skipping

Standard rope skipping is an excellent general method of building leg strength and should be included at the start of every workout. Use a one-beat jump (only one foot or both feet together touching the ground between each revolution of the rope). Be sure you utilize the wrists only in turning the rope. Start with a 1 or 2 minute duration and work to increase the duration of the jumping time to 5 minutes.

FINGERS, WRISTS, ARMS, AND SHOULDERS

Improvement in overall strength in arms and shoulders is probably not so important as improving strength in muscles specifically utilized in volleyball skills. The skills of serving, spiking, and passing are all dependent on sufficient muscular strength in the arm and shoulder region. However, the single aspect of strength is only one of several factors that must be considered as improvement is sought. Power in skill execution is brought about by an increase in strength, an increase in range of movement (flexibility), and an overall improvement in timing and skill. Many female players, from international competitors down to class level, lack sufficient strength to execute skills demanding power, while many male players lack sufficient flexibility to properly perform some basic skills. The following suggestions are concerned with improvement of strength and flexibility in the fingers, wrists, arms, and shoulders.

Improving the Fingers and Wrists

Finger and wrist flexibility and strength are absolute necessities before you can completely master the above-the-face pass. Certain advanced skills such as the jump set (to be described in detail in Chapter 7 on advanced skills) depend almost entirely on the hands and wrists. Although it is true that you do not need to spend a large amount of time on these areas, you must be fairly regular in including some exercise for the fingers and wrists in your workouts.

Finger and wrist flexibility

With your left hand, push on the extended fingers of your right hand, attempting to decrease the angle between the back of the hand and the wrist. Apply sufficient pressure on the fingers to feel a stretching sensation as you hyperextend the hand and wrist. Repeat three or four times for each hand.

Finger tip push-ups

By doing normal push-ups with only the finger and thumb tips touching the ground instead of the full palms, you will help develop finger and forearm strength as well as shoulder strength. Female participants unable to perform normal full-extension push-ups should use knee-position push-ups but still utilize the finger and thumb tips instead of the full palm and fingers. Begin with a sufficient number of repetitions to bring about some fatigue in the affected regions, and then increase the number of repetitions in succeeding workouts.

Extended arm hang

Utilize any overhead hanging type structure, such as a high bar, overhead climbing ladder, or stall bars. Grasp the bar with both hands and allow your full body weight to hang on your fully extended arms. A 1-minute hang at the onset of each workout will serve the dual purpose of increasing the flexibility of the shoulder region and the strength of the wrist–forearm area as well as stretching the muscle fibers to be used in powerful contractions during spiking and serving.

Inward shoulder rotation

Lie on your back on a table or bench, in such a manner that one shoulder and arm extend beyond the supporting surface. Extend the upper arm at right angles to the body and rotate the lower arm to a palm-up position at a right angle to the upper arm (as if you were raising your hand to ask a question). Place a nominal weight (15 to 20 pounds) in your extended hand, and using only elbow extension and shoulder rotation, raise the weight to a vertical position and then return it to a position slightly past horizontal. Repeat the exercise 10 to 12 times for each arm. The amount of weight may be increased or decreased as the need arises.

Shoulder pull-overs

Lie on your back on a table or bench so that your shoulders are supported but your head hangs over the end of the supporting surface. Extend the arms fully above the head and have another person place a bar of approximately 15 percent of your body weight in your hands. Using shoulder extension, raise the weight to a vertical position, directly over the head. Lower the weight, keeping the arms straight, back to the original horizontal position and repeat the exercise after a pause. Ten to 12 repetitions with the correct weight will suffice (for women it may be less) in a given workout to help increase shoulder girdle strength and flexibility.

WARM-UP

Each player should ensure that a routine warm-up procedure is instigated before each workout or competitive match. This warm-up should be of sufficient duration to prepare you to take part in skill drills or games without risking injury. In general, jogging, jumping, and stretching exercises should be included. Try to select activities that include all body segments at some time during the warm-up period. Specific mention should be made of the importance of stretching and aligning the lower back region.

Sacroiliac equalizer

Lie on your back with your legs together and flat on the ground and your arms fully extended to the side, palms down. Slowly raise your right leg to a vertical position, keeping the knee straight. Rotate the hips so that your right leg is allowed to extend as far as possible toward your extended left hand. In this position your leg will be straight and fully extended across your body, touching the ground as close as possible to the back of the left hand. After a short pause, raise your leg to a vertical position directly above the hip joint and then slowly lower your leg, still fully straight, to its original position. Repeat the exercise using the left leg and extending it toward the right hand. Be sure that your leg is raised to a vertical position before hip rotation brings the leg across your body. Also, make sure that after touching the ground near the back of your outstretched hand, you again raise your leg to a vertical position before returning to the starting position. Repeat the exercise three times for each leg.

4 □ Beginning Skills

THE SERVE

While the game of volleyball is a unique sport in many ways, it is similar to most forms of athletic endeavor in one very important aspect. To win and win consistently a team must make fewer errors than its opponents. Since only the serving team may score in volleyball, an error on the serve is an error that must be avoided. Many teams playing top level tournament volleyball feel that the number of serving errors must be kept at a minimum before winning is possible. Even in the most basic beginning classes, instructor and players are aware of the futility and loss of time in a game in which there are numerous serving errors.

As individual players gain skill in all phases of the game, it becomes obvious that the serve must be regarded as an important opportunity to score points for the offense. A player should develop a style of serving that is error-free and yet creates sufficient reception difficulty for the opponents.

Serving Skill

Every player must learn to get the ball consistently into play legally and effectively. Refinement of technique through regular practice is a must for the beginning as well as the advanced player no matter what serving method is employed.

The rules of the serve are the same for each type of serve to be considered. You, as a server, must be within 3 meters of the right boundary line and behind the rear service line. You may not contact the back service line on the court until after the ball has been struck by the hand, fist, or arm. To be a legal serve, the ball must not contact the net and either be played by an opponent or land inside the opponents' court. All boundary lines are considered "in bounds" in volleyball.

Finally, one very important and often neglected phase of consistent serving is proper mental set. As a player rotates into serving position, he or she should be formulating a definite plan of attack and preparing mentally for the serve. Many players use some specific action, such as locating the valve stem on the ball and placing it to the rear of the ball or straight up, as a reminder to pause and prepare mentally to serve.

Underhand serve

The most basic serve for beginning players of both sexes is the underhand serve. Although it is true that there are more effective serves and more spectacular ones, the underhand serve, once properly learned, is seldom "netted" or served out. Figure 4–1 shows the proper sequence of action necessary for a correct underhand serve.

When preparing to serve, stand facing the net with your feet staggered about toe to heel, with the foot opposite your serving hand forward. Bend forward slightly at the waist and place most of your weight on your rear foot. Hold the ball in the palm of your nonserving hand, with the arm fairly straight and extended across your body, to a point directly in front of your hitting hand. Address the ball with your hitting hand, palm toward the net. By swinging your arm in a controlled arc without actually striking the ball you will be able to check the position of the ball and your hitting surface in relation to the ball.

The hitting surface of the hand may be either a clenched fist or a semifist as shown in Figure 4–2. The semifist is made by simply doubling the fingers at the first and second joints and keeping the third joint straight. In either position, it is very important to keep the thumb to the outside of the first finger rather than bringing it over to touch the second finger as you would in a normal tight fist. By assuming the position described previously, having the hitting surface of the fist lightly touching the ball at a point behind and slightly below its center when

TABLE 4–1   Common Errors in the Underhand Serve and Corrections

COMMON FAULT	PROBABLE RESULT	CORRECTION
Standing sideways to the net	Ball is served into the net or out of bounds	Face the net with your body, and keep shoulders parallel to the net
Swinging side arm at the ball	Ball is hit into the net — lacks height	Swing hand and arm in a short controlled arc back and then forward to hit the ball
Making contact with the wrong location on the ball	Ball is wildly and inconsistently served	Make sure correct body and arm positions are being employed
Throwing ball wildly into the air before attempting to strike it	Ball is contacted too high or too low, resulting in a serve that is too low or too high	Release the ball only an instant before making contact — almost hit it from the holding hand
Failing to return the hitting surface to the address position	Ball is served to either side and out of bounds	Make sure the short forward motion of the hitting arm brings the hitting surface back to the address position at contact

Figure 4–1. Correct action for underhand serve.

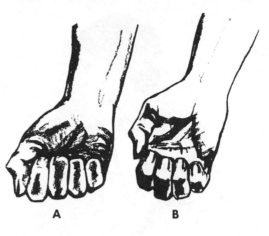

Figure 4–2. Correct hand or fist position for underhand. *A*, Fist. *B*, Semifist.

A B

held in its extended position, you are ready to start the serving action. Figure 4–3 shows the proper address position of the clenched fist and the ball.

As you take a short step toward the net with your forward foot, take the hitting hand and straight arm back in a line directly perpendicular to the plane of the net. As you complete the step, the hitting hand and arm come forward with sufficient force to propel the ball over the net. Try to return the striking hand to the same point on the ball which you assumed in the ready position. The arm and hand holding the ball should remain steady, and the ball should be dropped an instant before it is struck, not thrown wildly into the air and struck.

Overhand punch serve

The serve most commonly used by intermediate and advanced players is the overhand "punch" or "floater" serve. This serve is so named because of the arm action used in striking the ball and the resulting motion of the ball. While the punch serve is not so spectacular as the roundhouse or "spike" serve, its action approximates that of a knuckleball in baseball, creating a high degree of reception difficulty. Before attempting to master this serve, precise understanding of the nature and effects of the ball's trajectory and lack of spin on the ball is desirable. The correct trajectory is flat or parallel with the floor until the ball reaches the opponents' court at which time its loss of forward momentum begins. At that time, a complete lack of spin on the ball will cause it to react to any air currents in the playing area, bringing about a sudden dipping or darting of the ball.

Figure 4–4 shows a correct sequence of body movements to complete the punch serve.

When attempting this serve, you must concentrate throughout its execution from the time you prepare to serve until the ball is on its way. Face the net with shoulders parallel to the net and feet staggered in a toe-to-instep balanced position. The foot opposite the hitting hand is forward. The body is held in a nearly

Figure 4–3. Proper address position for underhand serve.

erect position as you prepare to put the ball in the air. Hold the ball, palm up in the nonhitting hand, in a position in front of the face so that the top of the ball is just below eye level. As you hold the ball in this position, address the ball with the hitting hand directly behind the center of the ball.

Your hitting hand is very important in the successful execution of this serve. The hand should be cupped as shown in Figure 4–5 with the finger tips together and the thumb touching the first finger near the outside of the second knuckle. The wrist of the hitting hand is held stiff, creating a rigid surface from elbow to finger tips. Note that as you lightly address the ball, contact is made with pads of the fingers, edges of thumb and little finger, and the heel of the hand.

From the ready position, you are confronted with the simple, yet important, task of correctly tossing the ball into the hitting area. Throw or lift the ball 3 to 5 feet in the air slightly in front of your body and directly in front of the shoulder of your hitting hand. As you toss the ball in the air, take a short step with your leading foot. Exact control of the ball in the air is important for consistency in executing the punch serve.

The hitting hand and arm are drawn back from the ready position as the ball is tossed so that the elbow is shoulder high and the upper arm is fully extended away from the shoulder. The hand and wrist should now be in a cocked position near your head. The forward arm action approximates the snap throw of a catcher to second base. Your elbow leads, swinging around in a throwing motion

Figure 4–4. The punch serve.

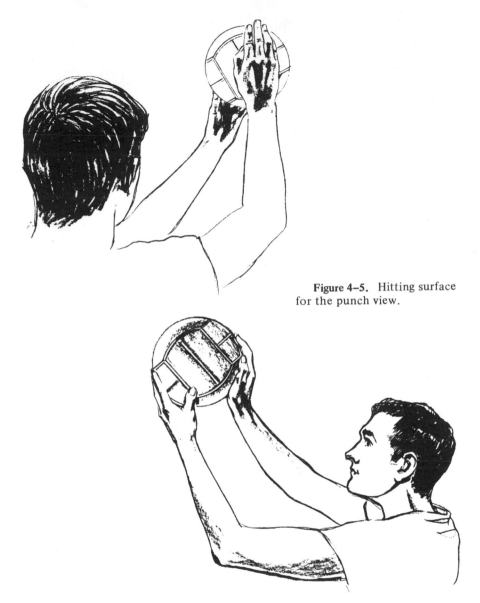

Figure 4–5. Hitting surface for the punch view.

to a point directly in front of the shoulder. As the elbow moves forward, the wrist and hand "punch" forward to contact the ball in the hitting area. After contacting the ball, follow through by abruptly stopping the hand and arm with a snapping motion.

TABLE 4–2 Common Errors in the Punch Serve and Corrections

COMMON FAULT	PROBABLE RESULT	CORRECTION
Striking the ball slightly below its center of gravity	Ball has underspin – does does not float	Hit the ball directly from behind its center of gravity
Striking the ball with insufficient force	Serve hits the top of the net or goes into the net	Hit the ball with sufficient power to ensure a flat trajectory on the ball until after it crosses the net
Extend hitting arm above the head	Ball travels in downward trajectory and contacts the net	The hitting arm should be brought forward from a cocked position, hand behind the head
Hitting the ball in an upward direction	Ball is consistently out of bounds – too long	Strike the ball behind its center of gravity with a level punch motion
Hitting the ball too hard	Serve is consistently too long	Strike the ball with less force (sometimes results in more floating action also)

Practice hints — points of emphasis

Underhand serve
1. Be mentally prepared to serve.
2. Have a definite serving strategy in mind.
3. Face the net.
4. Stagger feet — opposite foot forward.
5. Bend forward at the waist.
6. Hold ball across body with arm fully extended.
7. Be sure thumb is on the side of either fist or semifist.
8. Make a club of hitting arm.
9. Step toward net with forward foot.
10. Keep follow-through to a minimum.
11. Keep your eye on the ball until after it is struck.

Overhead "punch" serve
1. Be mentally prepared to serve.
2. Have a definite serving strategy in mind.
3. Face the net.
4. Stagger feet only slightly — opposite foot forward.
5. Hold body fairly erect.
6. Address ball in front of face with cupped hand.
7. Step forward with front foot.
8. Toss ball in controlled movement in front of hitting shoulder.
9. Cock hitting arm.
10. Bring hitting surface forward with throwing motion.
11. Keep follow-through to a minimum.
12. Keep eye on ball until after it is struck.

Drills

There are two drills used in serving practice that can provide a maximum number of individual attempts for the number of courts and volleyballs available. Figure 4–6 shows a typical court set-up involving 12 players and four volleyballs.

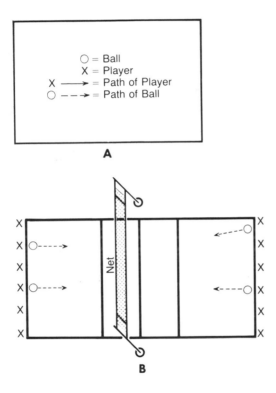

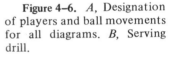

Figure 4–6. *A*, Designation of players and ball movements for all diagrams. *B*, Serving drill.

The players are divided into two equal groups and are dispersed along the base line of each court. Balls are simply served back and forth as they are caught or retrieved. Players should remember that the regulation concerning the 3-meter serving area is being relaxed to facilitate practice. Each server should be able to master the underhand serve before attempting the punch serve. Mastery of a serve includes consistency in getting the ball legally in play as well as accurate placement.

A second and slightly more advanced drill involves serve reception as well as serving practice. Although the total number of practice serves attempted is restricted, this drill does provide actual practice in serving to weak receivers or weak positions as discussed in the section on strategy. Figure 4–7 shows the actual location of players on the serving team.

The position of the receiving team may be varied as the instructor dictates. In this drill, the ball is served only from the 3-meter serving area and only by one

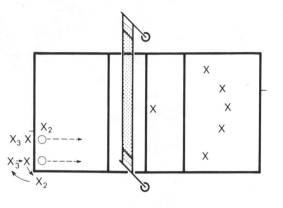

Figure 4-7. Combined serving and receiving drill.

player at a time. There are actually two sets of three servers. Player X is one of two alternating servers. Player X_2 acts as a retriever and a feeder to player X_3, the net server. The arrows show the rotation of the three players in the set.

THE PASS

Of all the fundamental skills necessary for the participation in the modern game of power volleyball, none is more important than the basic "above-the-face" (set) pass. This pass is so named because of the position in which the ball is contacted (see Fig. 4-8).

Skilled, experienced players use this pass almost exclusively for one purpose, "setting up" the offensive spiker. To be effective the set demands almost complete control of the ball in height, distance, and placement. Because of the amount of accuracy necessary in placing the ball in the proper "spiking zone" with regularity, many excellent players devote a great deal of practice time to this basic maneuver.

Beginning or inexperienced players should attempt to bring their skill levels in handling the set pass to an acceptable point in a short period of time because of the various play situations in which the above-the-face pass may be used. One of the probable uses of this pass is in receiving the high, easily played ball that crosses the net from the opponents' court without having been spiked. Another use of the basic pass is found when the ball has been poorly played by teammates (possibly attempting to set the spiker) and must be placed over the net on the team's third hit. Finally, as the individual skill level increases and the teamwork that is necessary for successful volleyball begins to develop, players use the basic set to place the ball high and near the net so that the ball may be spiked by a teammate.

Although it is true that the modern game of power volleyball gives the overall advantage to the taller player, players of below-average height have made themselves valuable to their team because of their ability to set a ball into the desired spiking zone with great regularity. The great "setter" as he or she is

Figure 4–8. Above-the-face pass.

sometimes called, has a very large part in determining the offensive success of a team.

Probably the greatest skill gap between the expert and the beginning player may be found in the ability to properly execute the basic set pass. The expert player is able to propel the ball in a graceful, almost effortless manner while the first attempts of the beginner seem to be mistimed, lunging efforts. The graceful set pass of the advanced player, however easy it may seem, is based on a solid foundation of knowledge, proper technique, and many hours of practice. Knowledge of the fundamentals of the set pass is imperative before such practice is beneficial.

Passing Skill

Young girls and boys in early elementary school master the technique of catching a ball thrown in the air. Without realizing the complexity of such movement, they are learning to anticipate the path of the ball and to place the body in a position to catch it. This sense of anticipation is important to the quick movement necessary on a volleyball court. You must learn to move under the ball in order to make a correct pass. The proper body position is such that if you did not interfere with the path of the ball, it would strike you on the head.

Once you have moved to a proper position under the ball, the placement of your feet and the action of your legs play a definite part in executing the basic pass. Figure 4–9 shows the correct position of the feet and legs in a slight stagger with both knees flexed. Often the beginning player tends to neglect the important role played by the lower body, so make sure your feet and legs are in the correct position.

The arms, wrists, hands, and fingers have the dominant role in making a good basic set pass. Figure 4–10 indicates the proper sequence of action of body segments when executing the basic set pass.

Note that you must have the elbows above shoulder height with the wrists extended as far back as possible. The ball should be played on the pads of your fingers and thumbs, not the fingertips or palms. To check this basic arm, wrist, and hand position, simply simulate a basketball chest pass without actually releasing the ball. With the ball held at arm's length in front of the body at the point where a chest pass would be released, rotate the arms above the head,

Figure 4–9. Position of feet and legs for basic pass.

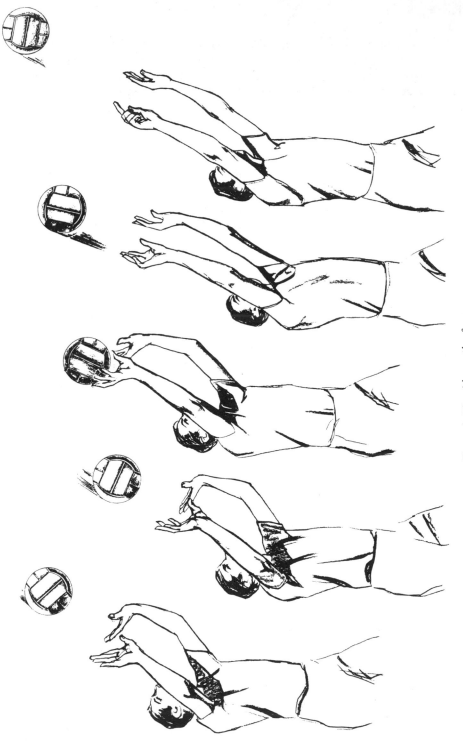

Figure 4–10.   Above-the-face pass.

elbows bent, and wrists rotated back to bring the ball directly above the face. The fingers are spread fairly wide and are relaxed. The hands are approximately 4 inches apart, measured between the ends of the thumbs. You should be in the correct position, directly under the ball, feet set, knees bent, arms and hands extended upward before the ball arrives whenever possible. Initially, face the direction you wish the ball to go.

The actual set should be a progression of movement involving the body segments. As the ball settles into the hands, let your fingers and arms "give" slightly to absorb part of the shock of the ball's downward force. The knees initiate the upward movement of the ball as they begin to straighten. Your fingers, wrists, and arms now complete the action of the pass by acting as springs to give the ball its upward momentum. You will generally be able to determine the improvement in your passing skill by two criteria: The ball should consistently travel in the trajectory you desire, and at the moment of contact there should be almost no sound.

The set

In power volleyball the "set" is simply an application of the "above-the-face" pass. It is performed by any player attempting to pass the ball at the desired height to a teammate positioned at the net so that it may be spiked into the

TABLE 4–3 Common Faults in the Pass or Set and Corrections

COMMON FAULT	PROBABLE RESULT	CORRECTION
Failure to set feet	Ball is not squarely met — lacks power and accuracy	Move rapidly to spot under the ball in order to have time to plant your feet
Failure to bend knees	Ball lacks height and accuracy	Plant your feet and assume flexed knee stance
Leaving the feet (jumping) before contact with ball	Flight of ball is inconsistent or lacks height — slapping sound is heard	Establish a good base and use legs to help propel the ball
Slapping at ball or making "paddles" out of hands	Inaccurate flight of ball and slapping sound at moment of contact	Spread your fingers and "give" with the ball at moment of contact
Elbows held below shoulder height	Ball fails to go forward — travels straight up or spins off behind passer's head	Make sure elbows are well above shoulder height when waiting for ball to descend
Reaching for the ball	Ball lacks height, direction, or distance	Wait for the ball to come to you — don't reach
Not facing in direction of set	Ball does not reach optimum spiking zone — too far back from the net or over the net into opponents' court	Plant your feet in such a manner that you are directly facing the desired path of the ball

opponent's court. The ball should be passed so that its downward flight is almost vertical at a distance of 1 to 3 feet from the net. The skill of setting the ball is almost identical with that of the above-the-face pass. Two aspects of normal passing skill should be emphasized by the player attempting to set the spiker: You must move rapidly under the ball and get your feet set in the staggered position, and, initially, you must face directly the desired ultimate destination of the ball.

The Bump Pass

The bump pass in volleyball describes the action used in playing the ball below chest height while utilizing both arms and clenched fists. There are two distinct play situations in which the bump pass is employed. In the first situation, serve reception, almost 100 percent of all serves are received by accomplished players by the bump-pass method. Beginning players should begin to receive as many serves as possible by this method and, as skill increases, attempt all serve receptions by utilizing the bump pass. The second situation in which the bump pass is employed is action in which the ball never gains sufficient height to be fielded by the player above chest height. The latter type of play utilizing the bump pass is frequently considered a "last chance" or emergency type of play. It should be noted that at no time is it considered legal to play the ball with the open hand below chest height.

Bump-pass skill

If you have time to move to a position directly behind the ball, it is desirable to do so. If no movement of the feet is possible, the ball may be played at the side of the body by turning at the waist and flexing the knees. In either case the feet should be planted parallel with the weight on the balls of the feet and the knees fairly deeply flexed, possibly as much as 90 degrees.

Your hands may be clenched or joined in several ways. Probably the most common method of making sure the hands are together is shown in Figure 4–11. Note that a fist is made with your left hand with your thumb on top. The right hand then encircles your left so that your thumbs are parallel and touching. Since the ball will be contacted most often by your wrists or forearms, it is important to have correct arm position. Hold your arms as close together as possible with the elbows straight and rotated inward. Try to make as flat and wide a surface as possible from thumbs to upper arms. Pointing your thumbs at the floor will help ensure a correct straight arm position. Figure 4–12 shows the correct position of the arms and body when waiting to bump the ball.

As the ball approaches, watch it until contact is made with the wrist or forearms. Again the legs provide the initial movement to provide force to start the ball up and away. Since the rebounding momentum of the ball off the forearms will provide force of its own, the only action necessary by your arms is a lifting action. An upward flowing motion of legs, shoulders, and hips as the ball

Figure 4–11. Close-up view of hands and arms in bump pass.

is contacted is desirable. Figure 4–13 shows the proper sequence of leg and arm action as the ball is bumped. Note the straightness of the arms at the elbow at the moment of contact and the force provided by the legs. Much practice is necessary in order to ensure the desired control of the bump pass.

Figure 4–12. Position of body and arms in bump pass.

Figure 4–13. Proper sequence of body segments in bump pass.

TABLE 4–4 Common Faults of the Bump Pass and Corrections

COMMON FAULT	PROBABLE RESULT	CORRECTIONS
Failure to have arms together	Ball flies off to side of desired trajectory	Rotate shoulders inward in front and attempt to touch elbows
Failure to have arms straight from thumbs to upper arm	Ball spins off to the rear, over player's head	Clasp hands together – rotate elbows inward and lock elbows
Swinging vigorously at ball with arms	Ball is not controlled or is hit out of play	Lift the arms rather than swinging them
Bumping the ball stiff-legged	Ball is not *softly* played or is played inconsistently	Play low to the ground by bending the knees
Not watching the ball	Ball is poorly placed or missed altogether	Watch the ball "on" to your forearms

Practice hints — points of emphasis — pass and bump pass

The pass
1. Move quickly under the ball.
2. Feet slightly staggered — well planted.
3. Knees are flexed.
4. Raise hands and arms and be ready before ball arrives.
5. Keep the elbows higher than the shoulders.
6. Hyperextend wrists — spread fingers.
7. Wait for the ball to come to you.
8. Give with the ball with fingers, arms, and wrists.
9. Initiate upward movement with legs.
10. Follow through, up and out.

Bump pass
1. Bend your knees — get low.
2. Get directly behind the ball whenever possible.
3. Clasp hands together, thumb on top.
4. Keep arms straight.
5. Hold elbows as close together as possible.
6. Watch the ball until it contacts your arms.
7. Try to play the ball on the wrists or forearms.
8. Lift with the entire body — legs initiate the action.
9. Keep the action flowing smoothly.
10. Follow through.

Drills for the Pass and Bump Pass

Since the bump pass is often employed for the same basic purpose as the above-the-face pass, one basic drill is used for practice in both skills. Figure 4–14 illustrates the basic circle formation; the arrows represent the possible path of the ball between players. Five or more players are able to use this drill effectively by stationing themselves approximately 6 feet apart on the circle. Any one of the players starts the drill by lofting the ball to any other player on the circle. This player moves directly under the ball and passes to any other player, with the exception of the player on either side of him. Emphasis should be on the necessity for facing the player to whom you wish the ball to go. The players

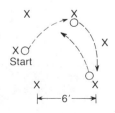

Figure 4–14. Circle drill for basic pass or bump pass.

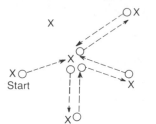

Figure 4–15. Circle drill with center pivot.

should be instructed to play the ball in the basic above-the-face pass unless it is impossible to get directly under the ball in which case the bump pass is used. Beginning players should be cautioned that the use of open hands in the below-the-chest pass should be avoided even if it means catching the ball and restarting the drill.

A slightly advanced variation of the circle drill is shown in Figure 4–15. In this drill, the same general procedure used in the circle drill is followed with the exception of placing a player in the middle of the circle. Any player remaining on the outside of the circle initiates the drill by passing the ball to the player in the center of the circle. The player in the center then passes the ball back to the player on the left of the original starting point. Each participant on the outside then receives the pass and returns the pass to the center player. This drill emphasizes the need to move the body into position rapidly and to face the desired direction of the pass.

A drill utilizing five or more players arranged in two single-file lines facing each other is used to familiarize players with the skill of passing the ball on the move (Fig. 4–16). The first player on either side of the formation starts the drill by passing a fairly low arched pass to, or slightly in front of, the first player in the opposite line. After passing the ball, the initial player moves to the rear of the opposite line. Each player in turn receives the ball as he or she reaches the front of his or her line, passes it to the player on the front of the opposite line, and moves to the opposite line. The lines should be established and maintained as nearly as possible during the drill at a distance of approximately 6 feet between the first players in the line. Should the ball be misplayed, the participants stop the action and resume the drill in a controlled manner rather than continuing in a pattern of poorly made passes.

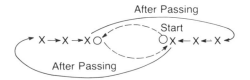

Figure 4–16. Moving pass drill.

Figure 4–17. Bump pass drill.

Bump pass drills

There are two drills in which the bump pass is emphasized as the sole method of passing the ball. In the drill illustrated in Figure 4–17, the player marked "A" (or the instructor) tosses the ball underhand below waist height, to the first player in the line of remaining players. The player receiving the toss attempts, by means of a properly executed bump pass, to return the ball 10 to 15 feet in the air to the original tosser. After bumping the ball, the player moves to the end of the line to await a second trial. It should be remembered that height and placement are both parts of a well executed bump pass.

The drill shown in Figure 4–18 is used to learn the skill necessary to return the ball over the net when it must be played by a player whose back is to the net. A player or instructor (marked "A") tosses the ball underhand to the first player in the line, whose back is to the net, standing at a distance some 8 to 10 feet from the net. The toss should be made so that it is slightly in front of the player whose back is to the net. The player receiving the toss attempts to bump the ball back over his or her head so that the ball clears the net and lands in the opposite court. After the first player attempts the pass, each remaining participant attempts the same pass and moves to the end of the line.

Figure 4–18. Over-the-net bump pass drill.

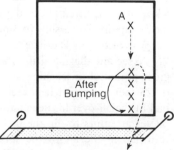

THE DIG

Often when playing balls that are hit just out of a player's normal reach or spiked balls that are traveling at great speed, it is necessary to employ an emergency method to reach the ball. The term used to describe the most common type of effort used to play the ball in this situation is "the dig." The dig consists of a one-hand effort to either side of the body with the arm extended fully in an attempt to reach the ball. It should be emphasized to players at all levels that receiving the serve or a hard-driven spike on either side of the receiving player is best achieved with a two-arm (bump-pass) effort, and that the one-arm "dig" is a play employed strictly when the ball is unreachable with both arms.

Digging Skill

Even though the dig is generally used in a last-second effort to keep a ball in play, it is possible to learn the mechanics of the dig under normal practice conditions. If the ball is coming on the right side, make a fist with the right hand with the thumb again to the outside of the first finger. Extend the arm and fist to a fully extended position, at the side of the body, with the finger side of the fist on top. Bend the knees to a semisquat position and have the weight slightly forward and on the balls of the feet. Figure 4–19 shows a player in correct digging position.

Attempt to strike the ball on the wrist but recognize the possibility that on a hard-driven spike, the fist, wrist, and forearm are all considered correct hitting surfaces. The amount of arm swing necessary will vary considerably with the amount of force supplied by the ball. If the ball is traveling in a straight line, as in a spike, little arm effort is necessary, but the knees are straightened on contact. If the ball is traveling in a less forceful manner, such as a misplayed serve reception, it will be necessary to add some upward force to the ball by an upward arm swing as well as the straightening of the knees.

Dig drill (Pepper)

The basic drill in learning the dig consists of simply having one player or coach toss a ball to either side of (and outside normal reach of) another player who, in turn, attempts to dig the ball in the air. By making the digging player move rapidly from side to side as the ball is tossed to alternate sides, the real purpose of the dig is utilized.

A second digging drill is a combination spiking and digging drill, but has great potential in teaching how to dig a forcefully hit ball. Two players stand 20 or 25 feet apart and face each other. One player begins the drill by tossing the ball in the air over his head and spiking it at or near the other player. The digging player attempts to dig the ball with the clenched fist in such a manner that it is returned in the air to the spiker to be spiked again to continue the drill. The

Figure 4-19. Proper position of arms and body for the dig.

player attempting the dig would soon realize that a low-to-the-floor, balanced position is necessary to permit rapid movement to either side.

THE SPIKE

There is probably no more exciting play in power volleyball, for spectator or player, than the basic offensive weapon of the game, the hard-driven spike. The skill of spiking is perhaps one of the more difficult sports skills to master because of the need to effectively execute and time the jump and proper arm action with the descent of the ball into the spiking area. In order to realize the importance

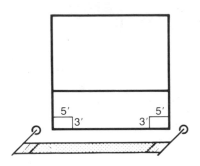

Figure 4–20. Optimum spiking areas.

of proper technique for the spike, players must be aware of the existence of the normal spiking areas at the net. This is an area on both sides of the net, approximately 3 by 5 feet in size, extending from the top of the net to the highest reachable point above the net. While the ball may be spiked in other locations, the side areas, as shown in Figure 4–20, are the basic areas for the successful attack play. The players on the offensive team at the left front and right front positions should always anticipate that the ball may be set into the spiking area and should be prepared to spike the set if it comes.

Spiking Skill

When the ball comes across the net into your court, you must move rapidly back from the net, 8 to 10 feet, and be alert for a set into your spiking zone. If the ball is set to you, make any necessary adjustment of a lateral nature before you start toward the net to contact the ball. This straight-in approach is necessary in order to provide a variety of shots and complete the proper recovery after spiking. The number of steps taken during the straight-in approach varies from player to player, but three or four steps would seem to be the average. Remember that the approach is important only to establish your position for the takeoff and to convert your forward momentum to upward momentum.

Take off with both feet from a balanced, nearly full-crouch position slightly behind the ball's path as it descends into the spiking zone. As you jump, thrust both arms violently upward to a fully extended position. You must be careful to jump as straight up as possible and not contact the net at any time during the spike.

When you are near the height of your jump, bring your hitting hand and arm to a cocked position with the hand behind the head and the elbow to the outside and at shoulder height. The hand is open and relaxed and the wrist is hyperextended. Try to contact the ball at the highest plane possible by extending the arm and hand in a striking motion. Keep the ball between you and the net and be sure that you contact the ball above its center of gravity with the open hand. Snap the hand and fingers forward and through the ball in order to direct the hitting force of the hand and arm in a downward direction. Figure 4–21 illus-

Figure 4–21. Proper spiking action.

trates the sequence of upper body, arm, wrist, and hand actions necessary in correct spiking procedure.

The proper follow-through of body segments after the execution of a spike is simply that of bringing the body and hitting arm under control to ensure a balanced landing on both feet. The momentum of the hitting arm should be halted as soon after contact as possible in order to keep from following through into the net.

TABLE 4–5   Common Faults in the Spike and Corrections

COMMON FAULT	PROBABLE RESULT	CORRECTION
Failure to jump straight up	Body or arm contacts net	Take off on both feet from crouch position
Jumping too early or too late	Ball goes into net	Time your jump to contact ball at maximum height
Running under the ball	Ball is hit out of bounds – too long	Keep the ball between you and the net
Hitting with closed fist	Ball cannot be properly aimed or controlled	Keep the hand open with fingers relaxed
Extending the arm without proper cocking action	Ball lacks sufficient force or speed	Cock the hitting hand and arm after you leave the ground
Failure to stop momentum of hitting arm after contact	Hitting hand comes in contact with the net	Stop movement of the hitting hand and arm abruptly after contact

Practice hints – points of emphasis – the spike

1. Start from a position three to four steps back from the net.
2. Approach the ball at right angle to the net.
3. Take off with both feet, knees bent to 90 degrees or more.
4. Thrust arms violently upward at takeoff.
5. Keep ball between you and the net.
6. Cock hitting hand and arm before reaching height of jump.
7. Snap the hitting hand up and out in a hitting motion.
8. Hit the ball with the open hand above the center line of the ball.
9. Hit the ball in a downward direction, over the net.
10. Stop the momentum of the hitting arm immediately after contact.
11. Land on both feet; bend knees to help gain balance.

Drill for the Spike

Before placing emphasis on team spiking drills, players desiring to master the spiking action must learn the proper hand and arm action. A simple wall drill may be used to learn and practice the correct striking motion employed in the spike. Utilizing time before or after class, a single player stations himself 15 to 20 feet from a blank wall with a volleyball. By simply throwing the ball into the air slightly in front of the hitting hand and then spiking the ball into the floor at a point some 10 feet from the wall, the ball will rebound on the bounce to a position where it may be spiked again on its descent. Care should be taken that the correct hitting action of the arm, wrist, and hand is employed, resulting in overspin on each spike.

A drill utilizing all players and both halves of the court may be used to advantage to learn spiking technique. For most players to properly learn spiking skill, the net must be lowered to a height only slightly higher than the reach of the average height player. This is a must for both sexes at beginning levels even if it necessitates lowering the net to 6 feet or less.

Figure 4–22 shows the correct formation of players on each court. One player or "setter" is stationed at the net in the middle of the front court with the volleyball. The remaining players are in a single-file line with the first player approximately 10 feet from the net and near the sideline. The player acting as setter tosses the ball in a two-hand underhand toss 15 to 20 feet in the air so that it descends into the spiking area. The placement of the ball is important to rapid learning of the spiking technique, and emphasis should be placed on the necessity of repeatedly tossing the ball high near the sideline and 1 to 3 feet back from the net. The first player in line approaches the point at which the tossed ball will descend, executes the proper takeoff and spiking action, and attempts to spike the ball into the opposite court. After the attempt the spiker moves under the net into the opposite court to retrieve the ball hit by the next player. After doing so the player goes to the end of the spiking line on that court.

For advanced players or players wishing to practice the spike the same formation is employed with a slight variation. The ball is started in motion by the spiker, who passes the ball to the setter, who in turn sets the ball at the desired height and depth so that it may be spiked. Net height for this drill should be maintained at the height that has been selected as the regular playing height.

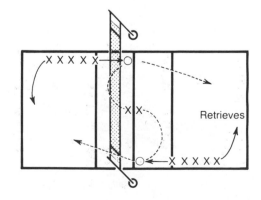

Figure 4–22. Normal spiking drill.

THE BLOCK

As the players in a volleyball group gain in skill, a logical increase in spiking skill results. Players on the defensive team find it necessary to counter the hard-driven spike or risk bodily harm. The most common method of defending a hard-driven spike is an effective block. Blocking rules and techniques in offensive play have changed in the past few years to the point that the normal block now involves only two players on the defensive team. In games involving beginning players, however, a block involving only one person is frequently effective because of the lack of spiking variations employed by the offensive team. Since a majority of the strategy involved in blocking is actually team strategy, only the physical actions of a single blocker will be considered here.

Figure 4–23. Correct blocking position.

Blocking Skill

As the set to the spiker is made in the opposite court, you must make an immediate decision if you are the player on the front line in the position to attempt the block. If you decide that the ball is placed accurately so that its descent will carry it near the net and fairly high and that the offensive player has sufficient skill to effectively spike the ball, you must attempt to block the ball. Figure 4–23 shows good positioning for a two-person block. As a blocker you have two possible objectives. First, you may try to simply block the ball back into the opposite half court, or, second, you may reduce the force on the spike so that the ball continues (in a playable line) into your own court where it may be set and spiked, placing your team on the offensive.

Whichever outcome you desire, as the ball nears the spiking zone in the opposite court, take off with both feet a distance of 1 to 2 feet from the net, taking care not to contact the net at any point in your jump. Extend both arms fully above the head, fingers and thumbs extended and fully spread. The hands should be fairly close together with the extended thumbs almost touching. The height of your jump will be determined largely by the opposing spiker. Generally, the more proficient the spiker, the higher you must jump.

The rule concerning the legality of going over the net on the block is subject to change from time to time. If the blockers are allowed to be over the net, by rule, your hands should be over the net whenever possible. The greater the penetration of the hands and arms over the net toward the ball, the more effective the blocker is in forcing the ball to the floor on the spiker's side of the net. It is illegal to touch the top of the net under any set the blocking rules unless the ball causes the net to contact the blocker.

Since the physical action of the block is little more than a simple jump and arm extension, it is obvious that to be an effective blocker you must have good timing and a knowledge of where to block. Timing is developed by watching the spiker approach the net, not the ball. Key your jump time by watching the spiker's takeoff time. Against a high jumper, delay your own jump slightly to

TABLE 4–6 Common Faults in the Block and Corrections

COMMON FAULT	PROBABLE RESULT	CORRECTION
Failure to move soon enough to blocking position	No block is employed	*Anticipate* the action of the setter — move to the ball rapidly
Jumping too early or too late	Block is ineffective	Time your jump to the hitter, not the ball
Coming down under the net after jumping forward	Foul at the center line	Jump from a position fairly close to the net and jump slightly up and back instead of up and forward
Blocking too far back from the net	Ball comes down on blocker's side of the net	Block with hands on or over the net

ensure that your hands are in blocking position exactly as the ball is spiked. Extend your hands and arms into a position to cover the flight of the ball whenever possible.

One final movement of the skillful blocker involves restraint rather than positive action. Frequently the block (or a dink shot) causes the ball to drop just behind the players executing the block. It is very important that the player or players involved in the block *do not reach back* to attempt to retrieve the ball in that location. A ball in play immediately behind the block should be recovered by a defensive player assigned specifically to that task.

Practice hints — points of emphasis — the block

1. Move rapidly to the spikable set.
2. Take off with both feet.
3. Jump up and slightly back.
4. Extend the hands and arms fully.
5. Time your block to the hitter, not the ball.
6. Try to have the spike strike the fingers and hands, not the arms.
7. Dominate the ball on the close set.
8. Don't reach back.
9. Do not contact the net or cross the center line completely when landing.

Drills for the block

In order to practice blocking, it is necessary to have repeated spikes with some degree of power from the opposite court. The best blocking drill is, therefore, directly associated with an active spiking drill. Once the spikers have some degree of confidence in their ability to spike, defensive blockers may be placed in the defensive court at the net. Any type of simple rotation involving spiking, blocking, and setting practice brings about a maximum amount of use from a single court. Players at all levels should be carefully observed during blocking drills; the need to stay out of the net during the blocking action should be emphasized. Since blocking over the net (when permitted by rule) brings about an increase in the tendency to touch the net (a fault resulting in a point or side-out), blocking drills should include the constant reminder to avoid contacting the net.

5 □ Rules and Scoring

Volleyball, like almost all organized team sports, has a lengthy and very definite set of rules and regulations concerning play. The United States Volleyball Association (USVBA) has been designated by the United States Olympic Committee as the National Governing Body in the United States and is the publisher of the rules and regulations used in most types of competition. The USVBA rules have also been accepted by the National Association of Girls' and Women's Sports and several affiliated organizations as the official rules governing play.

Since the entire rules section of the *Official Volleyball Guide* cannot be reprinted here because of obvious space limitations, this chapter will present a simplified discussion of the rules governing play, time factors, officials and their duties, and scoring considerations. The *Official Volleyball Guide* is published annually and is available from the address given in the Bibliography on page 109.

RULES

Teams and Players

A team shall consist of six players, one of whom shall be designated as captain. If during tournament play a team is reduced to less than six players by injury, the game shall be forfeited. (While the total number of six is fixed by rule during official play, the game may be played and enjoyed by fewer players during class or informal play.) Players are identified on the court by positions, e.g., left front, center front, or right back, but are not required to remain in the area of the court designated by those positions. They are, however, required to be in proper rotation order at the time of the serve and may not be in front of or behind their counterparts. (Center forward must be in front of center back, right back must be behind the right front, and so on.)

After the serve, all players may move to cover any portion of the court, with two exceptions: A back-line player may spike only if he or she takes off from a point clearly behind the 10-foot line, and a back-line player may not participate

47

in the block. All players must serve in the order established by their original position. As a team gains the serve, the new server rotates to the serving position from the right-front position and all other players rotate in a clockwise direction. This rotation must also occur the *first* time a team gains the serve if it did not win the right to be the first server. Line-ups may be changed for each new game; but once the game is started, players must remain in the same order for each serve. Substitutes may enter the game during deadball periods or time-outs. A player entering a game more than once must re-enter in the same place in the rotation that he originally occupied, and therefore cannot substitute for a player in a different place in the rotation.

Service

The team winning the toss of the coin before a match commences may choose to serve first or select the side of the court to be occupied during the first game. The team not serving first in the match serves first in the second game. The serve alternates in subsequent games. Each server of the team winning the serve continues to serve until the team commits a foul or the game is over. The player serving must be behind his rear boundary line and within the right side line. The server may not touch the line or the court until after the ball has been contacted, but a portion of his or her body may be in the air over the line. The ball must be struck with the hand, fist, or arm and may not be kicked or thrown. A served ball is dead and a side-out is declared if the ball:

1. Touches the net, a teammate, the ceiling, or any obstruction, or
2. Passes under the net or crosses the net over or outside the antenna, or
3. Lands out of bounds.

The server shall wait until the referees whistle or until the opponents are in position and ready to play before serving. If the ball is served before the opponents are ready, the referee shall declare a "quick serve" and shall direct the ball to be re-served with no point scored.

Net Play

A great deal of the total action in volleyball occurs at the net, and the rules governing net play are important. No player shall step completely *over* the center line with his or her foot. If any other part of the body such as a hand, leg, arm, etc., contacts the floor on the opponents' side of the center line, a foul is committed. The air space between the floor and the bottom of the net may be violated provided the net is not contacted and provided play is not interferred with on the opponents' court. A player may not contact the net during play even inadvertently. When the ball is driven into the net causing contact between a player and the net, no foul has occurred provided the momentum of the ball caused the contact. A player may reach over the net to block the ball, but the ball may not be attacked on the opponents' side of the net. A player may follow through over the net after spiking the ball as long as the net is not contacted and as long as the initial contact with the ball occurs on his side of the net. (Note: While the rules concerning net play permit players to be over the net during certain designated play situations, it is probably desirable to omit this rule for beginning players. Many times permittting the "over-the-net" rule to stand results in an overall degeneration of play brought about by a misunderstanding or disregarding of a distinction between over-the-net and in-the-net. As beginning players gain skill and an appreciation of the rules, the over-the-net rule may be reinstated and become a desirable part of total play.) The ball may be played from the net provided a team's three hits have not been used. The ball may legally contact the top of the net and continue into the opponents' court except on the serve. The ball must cross the net into the opponents' court in a path between the vertical antennae. (Any ball touching or passing over the antennae is considered out of bounds.)

Other Play

One of the more important differences between recreational volleyball and power volleyball is in the legality of the manner in which the ball is played in situations away from the net. In power volleyball the ball may not be struck with the open hand(s) when it is played below chest height or when it is played above chest height in any position except directly above the face. This situation indicates that, with the exception of the serve, the only time the ball may be contacted with the open hand is during the spike, the block, and the above-the-face pass. The specific rule governing the actual playing of the ball by a player states simply that the ball must be clearly hit.

Other rules regulating the manner of play state that the ball may not be played twice in succession, with three exceptions. Any player participating in the following situations may participate in the next play:

1. Simultaneous contacts by teammates
2. Successive contacts by a blocker
3. Simultaneous contacts by opponents

A player may leave the court to play the ball as long as he does not cross the center line. He or she may cross the center line (extended) during play, but may not play the ball while across it. A player may play the ball with any part of the body above (and including) the waist. A team shall be allowed a maximum of three hits to return the ball over the net. A play in which the ball is contacted by opponents simultaneously above the net shall not count as one of the team's three hits when the ball is next played by either team.

Conduct of Players

When a player is attempting to play the ball, opponents shall not shout at him or her or make any physical movement for the purpose of distraction, such as stamping their feet. Coaches and players are prohibited by rule from baiting any official or opponent by consistently questioning decisions or making derogatory remarks toward them. The referee has the right to declare a point or a side-out or to disqualify a player from the game when unsporting conduct is noted.

SCORING

Only the serving team may score in volleyball. A server continues to serve for 15 points or until his or her team commits a foul. The following are the main ways in which a point may be scored:

1. When the ball hits the floor of the opponents' court in bounds.
2. When the opponents fail to return the ball over the net in three hits.
3. When the opponents cause the ball to hit the floor out of bounds without having been touched by the serving team.
4. When any opposing player commits a foul (such as lifting or carrying the ball or contacting the net).
5. When the opponents cause the ball to strike an antenna or cross the net above or outside an antenna.
6. When the opponents cause the ball to hit any obstruction (wall, overhanging goal, referee's stand) before crossing into the opposite court.

A total of 15 points is required to win a game, provided the team gaining 15 has at least a two-point advantage. If a two-point advantage does not exist when one team reaches 15 points (15 to 14), play continues with no change of rules or scoring methods until the two-point advantage is gained (16 to 14, 17 to 15, 18 to 16). The referee does not announce "game point" when one team is within a single point of winning the game.

Play-over

In some situations, the referee shall declare the point to be replayed with no team gaining a point or side-out. These are:

1. When an official inadvertently blows his whistle during a live ball.
2. When a foreign object enters the court, interfering with play.
3. When a player is injured during a live ball.
4. When there is a double foul (players from opposing teams commit a foul on the same play, at the same moment).
5. When two opposing players hold the ball between them above the net.

TIME FACTORS

In certain instances it is desirable to include a time limit in a volleyball match. Each game consists of 8 minutes of live-ball action or 15 points. When timing a game, a timekeeper shall be delegated by the referee and shall sit with the scorekeeper opposite the referee. The timekeeper shall start the clock when the ball is struck on the serve, and the clock runs until the referee blows his whistle indicating that the ball has become dead. Only live-ball action is counted in the 8-minute game, and a team must be two points ahead when the 8 minutes elapse to be declared the winner. Additional time factors include a 2-minute intermission between games and two time-outs of a 30-second duration allowed each team per game.

OFFICIALS

There are five officials in a well conducted volleyball game (six — a time-keeper — if time is being kept), and each has important responsibilities for the overall conduct of the game. These five are the referee, umpire, scorekeeper, and two line officials. It is possible to play a game with fewer officials, but the burden placed on those conducting the game is greatly increased. While all officials have the responsibility of seeing that a game is conducted fairly and within the framework of the rules of the game, each official has specific duties.

Referee

The referee is the final authority in a volleyball game. The referee may make initial calls or overrule calls made by other officials (this rarely happens and should be done infrequently). His position during the game is at one end of the net, elevated in such a manner that he may sight down the net during play. The referee makes most decisions on the legality of hit or thrown balls, whether the ball is contacted on the block and whether any player contacts the net during a spike or block. As the ball becomes dead or a foul is committed to end each play, the referee shall declare a point, a side-out or a replayed point. The referee shall also rule on any matter not specifically covered in the rules.

Umpire

During a match the umpire takes a position on the opposite end of the net from the referee and remains at ground level. His responsibility is similar to that of the referee concerning the legality of hit or thrown balls, but his primary responsibility during play is ruling on plays at the net. The umpire should assist the referee on decisions involving the touching of the net by any player. Timing all time-outs allowed is the responsibility of the umpire, as well as timing the 2-minute allowance between games.

Scorekeeper

The scorekeeper shall take a position opposite the referee and shall be primarily responsible for recording the points scored as indicated by the referee. Usually, in tournament play, the scorekeeper also keeps score on any electric or mechanical scoreboard in use. The scorekeeper is also responsible for recording the original line-up positions and shall advise the referee or umpire on any situation involving an out-of-order rotation observed at the time of the serve. Substitutions and time-outs are also recorded by the scorekeeper.

Line Officials

Two line officials are stationed at opposite corners of the court. They have the primary responsibility for ruling on any ball landing near a line. (Balls landing on a line are considered in bounds.) In addition, line officials are frequently asked to rule on whether the path of a ball crossing the net is inside or above an antenna. Line officials are also expected to call any slight touching of the ball either at the net on a block or in the rear portion of the court away from the referee and umpire. Line officials do not make any judgment on the legality of hit or thrown balls.

6 ☐ Court Positions and Strategy

As in most team sports, volleyball has been developed into a highly technical, sometimes complicated, series of offensive and defensive maneuvers, feigns, and counterplays. As the skill and experience of those participating increase, so does the attempt to improve basic court coverage, attacking plays, blocking position, and so on. Although the early efforts by groups attempting to learn the game fall into a general "use whatever works" category, intermediate and advanced level teams are forced to adopt somewhat consistent patterns of play for given situations. The criteria for a basic team pattern of play is, therefore, twofold: (1) Is it effective? and (2) Can it be made to fit the large variety of play situations which develop during a contest? It is also necessary that players have confidence in whatever system is used. Confidence in a given system brings about several benefits to a team, including the obvious increase in performance when confidence is present. When players are confident that a system works, they are more likely to be consistent in carrying out their individual assignments, thereby bringing about an awareness by all players of correct court positions. Players are less likely to disregard assigned court coverage in an attempt to cover an area they feel is left unguarded.

There is a basic difficulty in attempting to designate specific instances of team strategy for isolated play situations. All teams are forced to adjust very rapidly from offense to defense and back to offense. If the serving team is considered the offensive team, then the team receiving the serve is the defense, but the basic reception of the serve is a vitally important part of the offense. Likewise, when the team controlling the ball has been able to give the spiker a high, wide set at the net and expects the spiker to leap and put the ball on the floor of the opponents' court, they must certainly be considered the offensive team. But even before the ball is spiked, players of the spiking team must move into positions to defend against a ball blocked back into their court, thus becoming defensive in nature. And even the block itself, the basis of good defense, is the first contact allowed the offensive team when the ball hits the block. Even with these conflicting situations in mind, it is still possible to outline a basic strategy based on court position for three main categories of play situations: (1) serve reception, (2) offensive positions and spike coverage, and (3) block coverage and free-ball coverage.

SERVE RECEPTION

It has been stated by many successful players that serve reception is the key to success in volleyball. With the perfection of the various difficult serves being used in today's volleyball, it has become apparent that if a team is to utilize the basic offensive patterns of play available to it, the reception of the serve must be accomplished in a skillful, controlled manner. Almost all basic offensive maneuvers are based on the assumption that reception of the serve will bring the ball in a high controlled arc to the middle of the front court at a distance of 3 to 8 feet from the net. Beginning players should be reminded that the two-handed bump is the accepted technique for handling a majority of serves.

Basic Beginning Serve Reception — No Switch

Since it is often advisable to allow each player to attempt skills at each position in order to determine who is best suited to spike, set, and so on, the basic serve reception position as illustrated in Figure 6–1 simply designates the middle man in the front row as setter (the player circled) as long as the team is on offense. The setter (C.F.) will make no effort to receive the serve in that position. The left and right front court players occupy the basic offensive spiking positions and are responsible for any ball served in an area within 5 to 7 feet of their respective side lines (see striped area in Figure 6–1). The center-back player (C.B.) in the diagram has the basic responsibility for all serves falling just over the net, but is relieved of any deep serve responsibility. The basic coverage responsibility of the center back is the shaded triangle in Figure 6–1. The back-court players, L.B. and R.B., have the deep serve responsibility between the shaded side zones as well as some short-serve coverage directly in front of them.

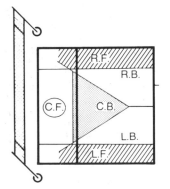

Figure 6–1. Basic position — receiving the serve.

The normal coverage zones of these back-line players is shown by the clear zones in Figure 6–1. All players attempting to receive the serve in this formation should be reminded that it is easier to react in a forward direction than it is to react backward and for that reason should assume an initial position slightly deeper than midway in their zone. Against teams still using an underhand style, it may be advisable to assume a position slightly forward of the basic position for reception of the more difficult serves.

Basic Serve Reception — Front-Line Players Switch

Since only the front-line players may spike the ball at the net, a player should be designated as a spiker or as a setter. It may become desirable to have two players designated as setters and four players designated as spikers in the overall offense. This is called the basic 4-2 offensive pattern of play. When using this system (probably the basic system of most intermediate and some advanced teams), the two setters are always inserted in opposite positions in the line-up so that one setter is always in the front row. When receiving the serve, if the setter in the front row occupies the left-front position, the serve reception alignment shown in Figure 6–2 must be used.

The ideal placement of the ball on the reception still remains the center of the front court, several feet back from the net. Thus, as soon as the opponents strike the serve, the setter in the L.F. court position moves rapidly toward the center of the front court, to become the setter. Again, it is important to note that the setter has no responsibility to receive the serve but simply moves rapidly to a position to set the ball to the spikers. It is also important to note that in lining up to receive the serve, the setter (L.F.) has lined up outside the center front (C.F.) player, thus maintaining the proper line-up rotation. Specifically, a player may not overlap with the player opposite him in a front and back overlap (center front must be forward of center back, left back must be behind left front, and so on) nor is overlap permitted with the player on either side in a lateral overlap position (left front must be outside center front, center back

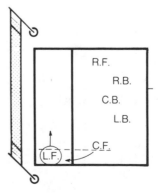

Figure 6–2. Serve reception — setter in left front.

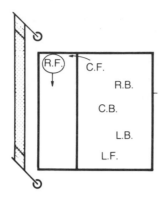

Figure 6–3. Serve reception — setter in right front.

must be inside right back, and so on). Reception responsibility remains the same as in Figure 6–1 except that the center-front (C.F.) player now assumes the coverage occupied by the left-front (L.F.) player in the basic coverage. Figure 6–3 shows the normal 4-2 offense serve reception when the setter has rotated to the right-front (R.F.) position. All responsibilities are identical to those designated in Figure 6–1 except that the center-front player covers the extreme right-side zone, and the setter now occupying the right front (R.F.) moves to the center of the front court as soon as the ball is served.

Advanced Serve Reception Positions

One of the more advanced offensive formations utilizes all six players as spikers as they rotate to the front line. This formation, known as a 6-0 formation, depends on the ability of five players to skillfully receive the ball, while covering a sixth player who will become the setter in the front portion of the court. Figure 6–4 shows the court coverage and movement of the right-back (R.B.) player when that player has been assigned setting responsibility. It must be noted that the players on the court in all serve-reception positions must retain the proper relationship in the lineup. Figure 6–5 shows the line-up for a 6-0

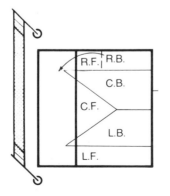

Figure 6–4. Serve position — right-back setter.

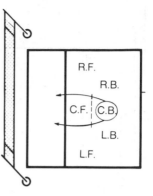

Figure 6–5. Serve reception — center-back setter.

system when the center-back (C.B.) player is designated as setter. The arrows showing the path of movement toward the front-court setting position indicate that from this position the setter may move toward the net by going on either side of the player covering him or her on the serve (C.F.). Since the logical placement of the serve will be toward the player moving to the set position, if the ball is served to the left side of the covering man, the setter moves toward the net by going on the right side of that player; conversely, if the ball is served to the right of the center front, the center back setter will move toward the net on the left side of the player in front of him or her. Figure 6–6 shows the line-up and path of movement when the left-back player is designated as the setter. Because of the ease with which the server may recognize the position of the left-back setter and attempt to serve the ball directly at the left-front (L.F.) player or even to that player's left in an attempt to "hide" the setter, the left-back player must be prepared to move toward the net on either side of the covering player. In all line-up positions the man designated as the back-court setter on a 6-0 offensive formation must move to the desired set location (center of the front court) as rapidly as possible. Care must be taken, however, to insure that the setter does not start toward the net *before* the ball is served, causing an official to call an overlap foul.

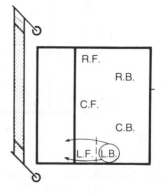

Figure 6–6. Serve reception — left-back setter.

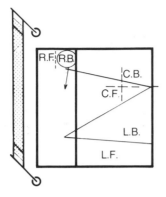

Figure 6–7. 6-0 serve reception – right-back setter.

6-0 Reception Formation with Two Players Up

As the skill of serve reception by individual players increases, it is sometimes desirable to attempt actually to receive the ball with four players, in order to allow the setter from the back court to be in setting position at the net at the time of the serve. Figure 6–7 shows the areas of court coverage by the four remaining players when the player in the right-back (R.B.) position has been designated as setter.

Several things should be noted concerning this formation. The right-back player (the setter) is positioned behind the right-front player and outside the center-back (C.B.) player, thus fulfilling the requirements of the overlap rule. The responsibilities of the remaining four players in court coverage are slightly increased. The center-front player still maintains a responsibility for a large percentage of short serves while the remaining three players, C.B., L.B., and L.F., have some short-serve responsibility but are primarily assigned to deeper court

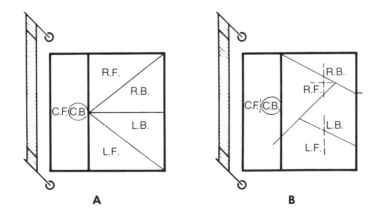

Figure 6–8. 6-0 serve reception. *A*, Center-back setter. *B*, Alternate method.

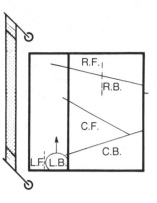

Figure 6–9. 6-0 serve position — left-back setter.

areas. Players must also be aware of their responsibility for the rotation in which the center back (C.B.) is designated as setter (Figure 6–8A). This is the most difficult of all the 6-0 serve reception formations. The right and left back (R.B. and L.B.) must assume a responsibility for a large percentage of all deep serves, including the difficult center-back deep serve, and the two front-line side players must cover almost all short serves, including those short and wide, even though they line up in a position side by side in the middle of the court.

One possible solution to ease this difficult coverage is shown in Figure 6–8B, in which the center-back player is still the setter but where the four remaining players alternate short and deep responsibility. In this reception formation, the right-front player is assigned a very large short serve area, and must take care not to overlap with the center back when taking the initial position. Figure 6–9 shows the correct court line-up and coverage areas when the left-back (L.B.) player has been given setting duty. This formation places a large area of coverage responsibility on the center front (C.F.) and right back (R.B.).

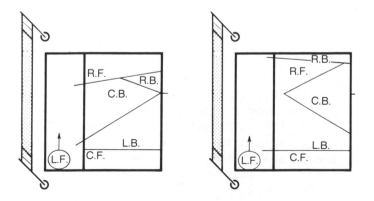

Figure 6–10. Serve position — covering weak player in right-back position.

Covering a Weak Receiver

Because of the value placed on accurate serve reception, it may be effective to alter any previously described serve reception formation in order to "cover" a player who is weak in receiving the serve. To do this a team will simply increase the area assigned to the receivers who are able to receive the serve while decreasing the area designated to the weak receiver. A team may also simply switch area assignments while maintaining legal positions to place a weak receiver in an area of less serve activity. Figure 6–10 shows how a team receiving the serve in the standard 4-2 formation might "cover" a weak receiver in the right-back (R.B.) position using either method of altering coverage.

OFFENSIVE POSITIONS AND STRATEGY

The basic offensive patterns used in a volleyball contest are generally simple attempts to utilize individual player talents as much as possible. The methods used to bring about this utilization vary in complexity and effectiveness as well as degree of deception. Beginning teams would do well to limit their offensive maneuvers to the simple fundamental progression of serve reception — set and spike — utilizing players showing particular talent for the set and spike. As skills increase, it may be desirable to initiate an offensive formation that offers some deception without sacrificing a great deal of dependability. Advanced offensive formations often utilize particular talents of individuals in a deception and effective attack combination. There are actually two areas of consideration in offensive formations: (1) the method and court position when attempting to receive, set, and spike the ball, and (2) the method and position utilized to attempt to cover the court during the spike in the event the ball is blocked by the defense at the net.

Basic Offensive Patterns

It is obvious that the offensive pattern used will depend a great deal on the type of serve-reception formation that is utilized. The basic offense for most beginning teams consists of simply trying to get the ball to the center-front (C.F.) player (the setter), who in turn attempts to set the ball to a position above the net to be spiked by either the left-front player (L.F.) or the right-front (R.F.) player. To ensure the probability of a reasonably well set ball, the setter should begin by passing toward the spiking area he or she is facing as the ball comes from the serve receiver. In effect, if the ball is received by a player on the left side of the court, the setter should attempt to set the left-front spiking position (See Fig. 6–11), and, conversely, the setter should attempt to set the right-front spiking position if the ball comes from the right side of the court on the serve reception.

Once the setter has reached the skill level necessary to be reasonably accurate with the over-the-head (flip-flop) pass, the offense may take on a basic deception quality. That is, as the ball comes from the serve receiver to the setter in the front-center court location, the setter may pass the ball to either spiker without necessarily changing the direction he or she is facing. If the setter chooses to set the spiker directly ahead, a basic above-the-face pass is used, but the setter also has the option of setting the ball overhead to the spiker behind. Teams generally designate the left-front spiker as the "on-side" spiker and the right-front spiker as the "off-side" spiker. This designation is given because on the left-front court the ball does not have to travel across the body of a right-handed spiker and thus is hit with the "on" hand. Whereas, when the ball is set to a right-handed spiker on the right front court, the ball must travel across the body to the "off" hand before it is spiked. The choice of whom to set is determined by the setter on the logical basis of who may be expected to "put the ball away" most frequently. When making this decision, the setter should consider the ability of the spiker, the location of the ball following the serve reception, and the personnel involved in the defensive block. The weakness of the basic system just described lies in the fact that the player occupying the center-front position is always designated to be the setter. Thus, a player talented as a spiker may be forced to set the ball to a left- or right-front court player who may have outstanding setting ability but who lacks the ability to spike. Since this situation is undesirable, teams with some degree of experience resort to a 4-2 offense (four spikers and two setters) involving a front-line switch of players, bringing the setter to the middle position (after the serve) and moving spikers to the outside front-line spiking position. Figures 6–2 and 6–3 show how this switch is accomplished on the reception of the serve.* This offensive switch also produces the more desirable spiking location. Figure 6–12 indicates how a line-up should be arranged in order to have setters (circled players), stronger spikers (S.S.), and

Figure 6–11. Basic offense.

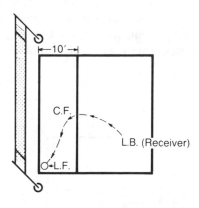

---

*When the switching team gains the serve, the switch of players is accomplished immediately after the server has contacted the ball.

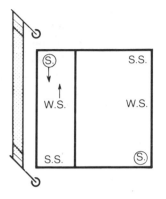

Figure 6–12. Basic player positions and switch; setter in R.F. ⑤, setter. W.S., weak-side spiker. S.S., strong-side spiker. →, player movement.

weaker spikers (W.S.) in the proper location. The arrows in Figure 6–13 indicate the switches that are necessary in bringing about final court positions for the first three positions using a 4-2 pattern. Note that in a line-up rotation in which the setter already occupies the center-front location no switch is necessary to bring about the desired player alignment (Fig. 6–14).

Spike Coverage — Basic Offensive Patterns

All teams must have a prearranged court coverage for the offensive-spike play. If the ball contacts the defensive block, three possible situations may result. The ball may go off the block and out of play; the ball may continue into the defensive court, in which case the spiking team players must move immediately into assigned defensive positions; or finally the ball may be blocked back into the offensive court. Offensive court coverage during the spike is an important part of the total offense, and all players must be alert for the blocked ball coming into their assigned court locations. Figure 6–15 shows the court assignments for a ball spiked by the left-front spiker. The setter (⑤) and the left-back players should be stationed in a crouched position very close to the spiker

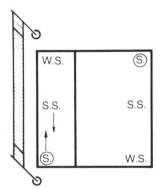

Figure 6–13. Basic player position and switch — setter in L.F.

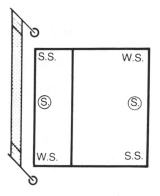

Figure 6–14. Basic player position – setter in C.F.

to take any blocked ball coming just over the spiker's head. (The spiker should never reach back for such a ball.) The right-front and right-back court players cover their respective positions, while moving toward the spike (see Fig. 6–15), and the middle-back court player is assigned any ball coming off the block, deep in the court. Each of the players covering the spike should be reminded that a ready position encompassing a very low center of gravity must be employed to enable the player to react swiftly to blocked balls coming into the player's defensive area.

Advanced Offensive Patterns

Teams with personnel containing a sufficient number of players who are both talented spikers and ball handlers may wish to use an offensive pattern involving six spikers (6-0). In a 6-0 system the offensive team is able to utilize all three front-line players as spikers. This is accomplished by having a back-court player come to the front line to act as setter when the team is on offense. Figures 6–4, 6–5, and 6–6 demonstrate how the back-line player moves toward

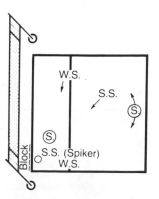

Figure 6–15. Spike coverage – 4-2 offense spike.

the net during the serve reception.* Once the back-line player has reached the desired front-court position and the ball is delivered to that location following an accurate serve reception, the ball may be set to either of the normal front-corner spiking zones, or it may be set to the middle spiker approximately at the center of the net. An obvious advantage is gained in that the defensive team is unable to determine quickly enough the location of the spike and thus produces an ineffectual block and poor court coverage. By varying the height and location of the set, the offensive deception is tremendously increased during the use of a 6-0 offensive pattern. Several items should be considered before attempting to use such a system. All players on the court must have the ability to receive serves, set, and spike, as well as fulfill all defensive requirements. The team using this system must also be aware that any inconsistency in getting the ball to the setter will result in a poorly executed attack. The overall defensive coverage is somewhat impaired following an unsuccessful attack. Players must be very well drilled in switching movements and court coverage.

Spike Coverage — 6-0 Pattern

The coverage of the offensive spiking play during a 6-0 pattern attack must consider two possibilities. The first of these occurs when the ball is set to either side spiking zone (Fig. 6–16). The setter and the left back cover the short return (when the spike is from the left side as indicated) and the middle-front spiker drops back to cover the mid-court area. The right-front spiker and the right-back court player cover any ball rebounding deep off the block in their respective areas. The second coverage necessary occurs when the ball is set to the middle spiker at the middle of the net, as shown in Figure 6–17. The setter and the two front-line corner spikers follow in to attempt to play any short ball coming off

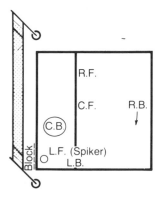

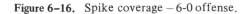

Figure 6–16. Spike coverage — 6-0 offense.

---

*Figures 6–7, 6–8, and 6–9 illustrate how a variation in reception position allows the back-court player to be in the front court during the serve.

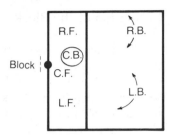

Figure 6–17. Court coverage — middle spike.

the block, and the two back-court players divide the back court area to play any ball coming deep off the block. The court coverage on the mid-net set is somewhat weaker than when the spike occurs at the normal side-spiking zones.

Combination Offensive Patterns

Many teams find that a combination of the 4-2 and 6-0 offensive patterns provides a more consistent offensive attack, while still providing a fair amount of deception. In the normal combination of the two systems, the setters are placed in opposite court line-up positions as in a 4-2 system, but they are required to spike the ball effectively on occasions from the center-front position. The offense operates normally as a 4-2 offense, with the majority of the spiking duty being handled by the two corner spikers and the setting responsibilities falling to the setter in the front line from the center-front position. The 6-0 condition of utilizing the middle player (normally the setter) as a spiker occurs only when the opposition is forced to return the ball weakly over the net in what is termed a "free ball." When the free-ball situation occurs (free-ball court coverage will be discussed in the next section of this chapter), the back-court setter moves immediately to the net and is able to set the ball to the middle spiker if it is desirable. It must be remembered that any system that utilizes a back-court player in the set position must make provision for that player moving to a defensive position once the ball has crossed the net into the opponents' court.

DEFENSIVE POSITIONS AND STRATEGY

A team is considered to be the defensive team whenever the opponents are engaged in playing the ball on their side of the net. Therefore, a defensive alignment must be formed by a team as soon as one of its players has served or as soon as the ball has passed over the net during any scrimmage play. There are three basic considerations given to defensive play: (1) the formation of an effective block, (2) court coverage by players not participating in a block, and (3) court coverage during a "free-ball" return.

Formation of the Block

Since back-line players are prohibited by rule from participating in the block, the three front-line players are responsible for forming and executing the block on any ball in position to be spiked by the offense. When defending against beginning offensive patterns or a 4-2 offensive pattern, the defensive team should be able to put two players on the spiker with some degree of regularity. Under these systems the player opposite the offensive spiker is responsible for positioning the block. This outside player, usually an offensive spiker (when his or her team has the ball), attempts to jump and position his or her outstretched hands so that the outside hand is directly in front of the ball with the inside hand adjacent to it. The middle player in the defensive front line becomes the second player on the block and attempts to position both outstretched hands and arms just inside the position covered by the outside player. Ideally, the four-hand barrier will prevent the straight-away power spike from hitting the floor and will encourage the spiker to hit a sharper angle shot, which may be picked up by back-court players. The middle player on the defensive front line is the key to a successful block. His or her ability to move rapidly in a lateral direction to get to the block will enable the blocker to perform effectively. In defending against a 6-0 type offense the middle player must stay in position in the middle of the front line in order to attempt a block of any ball set to the middle offensive spiker. When the ball is set to the middle spiker, either of the outside defensive players may be able to move to a position to help with the block and should do so if possible.

Court Coverage for Nonblocking Players

With the advent of the various offensive formation and the increased number of lower-set spikes, the overall effectiveness of the two-player block has been reduced. As a result, more and more emphasis is being placed on the positioning of the four players not involved in the actual block. These players should assume positions in which they have an opportunity to play partially blocked spikes, dink shots (softly played lob shots, just over the block), and spikes that go over or around the block. Figure 6–18 shows a normal defensive court coverage

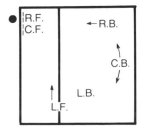

Figure 6–18. Defensive court position on the block.

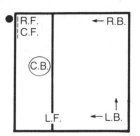

Figure 6–19. Court coverage — back-court setter covering close.

against a normal spike from the left-offensive front court. The coverage discussed below assumes that a tight, high block is made by the two players in the center-front and right-front positions.

The right back-court player has the responsibility for a ball tipped off the block or a dink shot falling just over the block. The player usually starts from a position 6 or 7 feet from the back line, fairly close to the side line. The center back player covers much of the deep court and attempts to play all balls coming deep off the block and deep lob spikes. He has deep right court dink responsibility. The left back court player is the primary digger — the player responsible for covering the angle of the ball hit just inside the block. He or she should be positioned some 8 to 10 feet from the left side line, depending on the ability of the spiker, and should be able to see the ball clearly inside the block. The left-front court player should drop off (back away from) the net and be prepared to start toward the ball as it is spiked from a position 4 to 5 feet from the left side line and 10 feet back from the net. The left-front court player is responsible for a spike hit inside the block on a very sharp angle, the ball glancing off the block to the inside, and the dink shot hit toward the center of the court. When using a 6-0 offensive system, the setter from the back court is frequently caught near the net when the team goes on defense. Figure 6–19 shows the correct court positions for all players when this occurs. All responsibilities are similar, except that the back-court setter (C.B.) attempts to play all dink shots from the close-in position behind the block. This defense is somewhat weaker than the defense shown in Figure 6–18 but must be used in certain circumstances. When the ball is set to and spiked by the middle spiker, all players must react as quickly as possible to try to reach assigned defensive positions. Figure 6–20 shows the positions

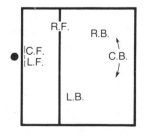

Figure 6–20. Defense coverage — middle spike.

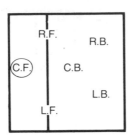

Figure 6–21. Free ball coverage.

of the nonblocking players against a center spike. This coverage assumes that the left-front player was able to reach the ball and help the center-front player in the block attempt. The right-front player assumes a position on the 10-foot line, 4 to 5 feet from the right side line, and is alert for very sharp angle hits and balls glancing off the block. The two back-court side players cover the angle shots immediately outside the block. Their position is approximately halfway between the net and the back line with R.B. slightly deeper than L.B. The center back player again has deep (back area) responsibility and must be prepared to move laterally in either direction.

Free-Ball Coverage

A free ball in volleyball is described as a play in which the offensive team plays the ball weakly over the net. Proper player position on a free-ball play is important to the team receiving the free ball because it enables it to start a new offensive thrust with a fairly simple accurate pass to the set player in the front-center position. When any player on the team receiving the free ball recognizes the situation on the opponents' court, the phrase "free ball" should be loudly proclaimed. All players should then move to the court positions shown in Figure 6–21. The key player in the reception of a free ball is the center back player, who must come forward from the regular deep position to a position approximately in the center of the court. Experience has shown that a fairly high percentage of free balls will fall in this area. (When playing a 6-0 offense, the center spiker should retreat to this center-court location and play the ball up to the back-line setter who has assumed a position at the net.)

The success of any of the defensive alignments discussed depends entirely on the ability of the players to recognize the correct position, get in position before the ball arrives, and play the ball legally and accurately in order to initiate a new offensive play.

7 □ Advanced Skills

Players of both sexes wishing to become more accomplished in the game must be willing to learn skills beyond the bare fundamentals of power volleyball. Participation in leagues, sports days, tournament play, and the like can be much improved by gaining a knowledge of technique and spending sufficient practice time to master a few advanced skills. It must be emphasized that the advanced skills to be presented here are in no way a substitute for the fundamentals, but are, rather, suggested for use in specific situations in which deception is desired or in which a basic skill is insufficient to meet the demands of a given play.

ADVANCED SERVING TECHNIQUES

The Roundhouse

Probably the most spectacular serve in power volleyball is the overhead-roundhouse serve. The mechanics of this serve demands that the ball be struck with a great deal of power at a point slightly below its midline to create a large amount of overspin, thus producing a fast, rapidly dropping serve. It should be noted, however, that because of the existence of the overspin on the ball, the ball tends to maintain a predicted trajectory, thereby making it simpler for the fielding player to control the reception. The roundhouse serve is more effective when used against individuals having somewhat less experience and skill than players at an advanced level. Many players master the skill of the roundhouse in order to use the mechanics during nonserving situations. A ball that must be played over the net on a third hit from deep in the court may be played successfully using roundhouse mechanics. Some players have also utilized this technique in spiking a ball that has been poorly set.

Roundhouse serving skill

Stand with your left side to the net (for a right-handed server), with your feet spread about shoulder distance apart. Since you will take a short step toward the net, assume a starting position far enough back from the end line to allow the step to be completed without contacting the end line. The toss of the ball by the nonhitting hand is very critical to the successful execution of this serve. The ball should be tossed in a lifting motion from a point directly in front of the chest to a position 8 to 10 feet directly above the head. As the ball descends, the hitting arm and hand are held in the starting position of arm pointing straight down, hand open, palm rotated out. The actual hitting surface is the open hand, fingers slightly cupped, wrist fairly stiff. The arm swing, with the arm fully extended, is timed so that the hitting surface of the hand is brought into contact with the ball at a point of full-arm extension, almost directly above the right shoulder. The short step taken toward the net by the left foot during the swing helps transfer the body weight to the left side and also allows the contact with the ball to take place above the right shoulder rather than above the head where the ball was originally tossed. The ball is contacted almost directly behind and slightly below its center of gravity. The hand and fingers follow through over the ball to impart the desired overspin on the ball. Since the normal path of the ball will be in a downward direction, the serve should be aimed at a point a few feet above the net. Figure 7-1 shows the correct sequence for a roundhouse attack on the ball.

TABLE 7-1   Common Faults in the Roundhouse Serve and Corrections

COMMON FAULT	PROBABLE RESULT	CORRECTION
Swing lacks power	Ball fails to clear the net	Roundhouse serve must be hit with powerful swing
Not putting overspin on ball	Ball goes out of bounds, too long	Follow through over the ball
Not tossing the ball high enough or with accuracy	Ball is poorly hit — lands out of bounds or in the net	Practice the toss until it can be placed where you want it
Failure to take short step with leading foot on swing	Ball fails to clear net	Take a short step with the leading foot (foot closer to net) as you swing

The roundhouse floater

A variation of the roundhouse, the roundhouse floater, has become a very common serve, especially in recent international competition. The roundhouse floater is very similar to the regular roundhouse so far as mechanics are concerned, but adds a new dimension to the effectiveness of the serve. The ball is struck with the flat of the hand, and a minimum of follow-through is utilized to create a floater-type action of the ball. As with the regular floater serve, the lack of spin on the ball causes its path to be unpredictable and therefore more difficult to receive. Two slight modifications in technique also are required to master the roundhouse floater. The ball must be contacted slightly in front of the body instead of directly overhead as in the regular roundhouse, and the foot closer to

Figure 7-1. Roundhouse technique.

the court must be dropped back from a perpendicular line to a position 6 to 8 inches behind perpendicular, creating a slightly open stance.

ADVANCED PASSING SKILLS

Once a player has mastered the basic above-the-face pass, it is usually a simple matter to learn to regulate the height and forward distance that the ball will travel. Several of the advanced spiking techniques demand that the pass or set have a definite predetermined height and distance from the net. In order to add deception to the set, most players attempt to master the back set or "flip-flop" set. This is a type of above-the-face pass that is carried out with much the same mechanics as the normal pass but in which the intended path of the ball is behind the passer. Figure 7–2 shows the successful completion of a back-set pass.

Back-Set Skill

You should review the basic above-the-face pass, including the part played by the feet and legs. The back-set pass is very similar to the basic pass except that the path of the ball is controlled in a backward flight. Once you have positioned the feet, legs, and body in proper location, check to ensure that the arms and hands are in correct position above the face. Be sure that you have taken a position directly under the descent of the ball. As the ball makes contact with the pads of the fingers, your legs have started to uncoil. Your arms play a major role in completing the back set. As the ball is contacted, the arms, acting like springs, start up and away from the body, but the shoulders now rotate slightly

TABLE 7–2 Common Faults in the Back Set and Corrections

COMMON FAULT	PROBABLE RESULT	CORRECTION
Body is not positioned directly under the descent of the ball	Ball is misplayed or fails to go in backward direction	Set the feet so that the ball descends directly above the head
Ball is contacted below face height by hands	Ball is carried illegally	Contact the ball above the face — particularly important in back set
Upper body lean is too far back, or arms travel too far back beyond head	Ball travels in flat trajectory — travels beyond normal spiking zone	Control upper body action and back motion of arms so that ball travels up and back
Ball is contacted behind the head	Ball travels in flat trajectory	Contact the ball above the face not behind the head
Upper body starts backward before ball is contacted	Deception is lost — opponents are aware a back set is coming	Wait to move upper body until ball is contacted

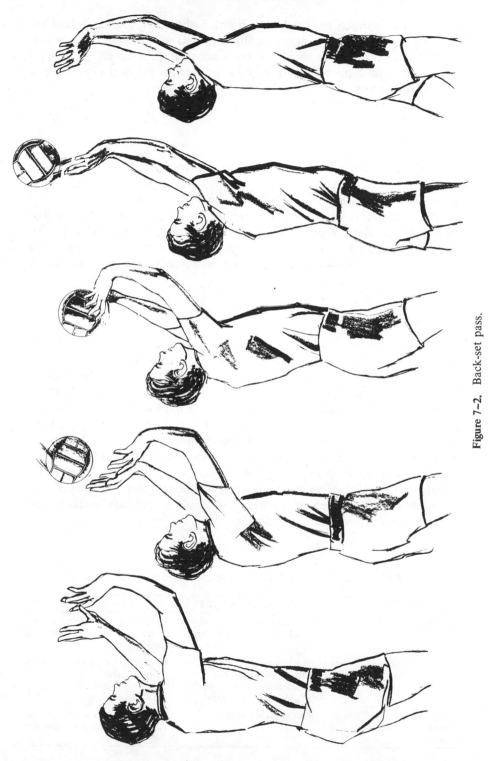

Figure 7–2. Back-set pass.

up and back, bringing the hands to a position above and slightly behind the head. Your upper body also moves slightly backward after the ball has been contacted by the hands. Care should be taken not to initiate the slight backward movement of the upper body until after you contact the ball or the deception of the play will be lost.

Jump Set

Many teams utilize a one-pass play to the spiker on a "free ball" situation. In essence, this play occurs when a softly played ball comes over the net to the spiker. The spiker then has two options, spiking the ball or resetting the ball to another front-line player to be spiked over the net on the third hit. Skilled players are able to add deception to the play by utilizing a jump set by the first spiker. The jump set is executed by the spiker in much the same manner as the above-the-face pass with the exception that the player jumps and is actually in the air when the ball is set.

Jump-set skill

Since the sole purpose of the jump set is to create deception, you must learn to make your jump resemble a normal spike jump. After leaving the ground, turn your body so that your shoulders are perpendicular to the net. The jump should be executed so that the head will be in a position directly under the ball's descending path. The hands and arms must provide most of the up and outward momentum for the ball, since the legs are not in contact with the ground and cannot help provide normal force for the pass. The action of the hands and arms is almost identical to that of the normal above-the-face pass, except that the ball should be allowed to drop slightly lower before contact is made, producing a slightly greater angle at the elbow, to create additional power for the pass. The overall timing of the jump set is critical and should be practiced under various play situations to ensure proper results.

TABLE 7–3   Common Faults in the Jump Set and Corrections

COMMON FAULT	PROBABLE RESULT	CORRECTION
Jumping too early	Ball lacks power because of lack of body momentum	Time your jump so ball is contacted at top of jump or slightly before
Failure to turn shoulders perpendicular to the net	Ball travels over the net into opponents' court in excellent position to be "put away" by them	Be sure to turn your shoulders completely
Jumping with shoulders already perpendicular to net	Reception is lost	Wait until you leave the ground to begin turning the shoulders

ADVANCED BUMPING AND DIGGING

It is necessary to develop the ability to keep the ball in play during all types of situations. This ability often is dependent solely on the skill of the individual player to play the ball under conditions that are less than optimum. One of the outstanding differences between United States players and foreign players during international competition in the past has been the ability of the latter to retrieve balls that were headed out of play by a diving, rolling, digging maneuver that saved the point or side out. Japanese men and women in particular are very adept at this kind of save. It should be noted that the diving type of save is considered a very advanced skill and should be undertaken only by those players having received training in the proper execution of the play.

Front-Diving Save

When the ball is about to drop to the floor in front of you at a distance beyond reach by a normal bumping procedure, you must learn to execute a front-diving save. Move toward the ball with short driving steps with the weight well forward. Take off at the last possible moment with both arms outstretched toward the path of the ball. Contact with the ball is made either with both hands and wrists in a cupped bumping position or with the back of one hand, wrist stiff. Since this is strictly a saving maneuver, try to play the ball high into the air in the direction desired. After contact with the ball, spread the hands, palms down, in preparation for contact with the floor. The primary shock of landing is absorbed by the hands, arms, and shoulders. Allow the arms to rotate from the shoulders in a backward and downward direction so that the initial shock is absorbed by the hands and arms. By arching the back the remainder of the force of landing is taken by the chest and upper abdomen in a sliding action. Figure 7–3 shows the proper cushioning of the landing after successfully saving the ball. Instruction and practice of the front dive and slide should be initiated on some type of mat and should not be attempted on the regular playing floor until the procedure has been mastered on the mat.

Side-Rolling Save

When the ball is out of normal reach of either side, it may be necessary to leave your feet in an effort to keep the ball in play. As in the front-diving save, it is absolutely necessary that sufficient instruction and necessary practice time have been devoted to learning the mechanics of the side dive and roll before it is attempted. When you are ready to attempt the play, take a short digging step with the foot toward the ball and push off in that direction with the opposite foot. Bend the knees before leaving your feet in order to help lower your center of gravity and have the torso leaning well toward the spot of anticipated contact. As you dive toward the ball, extend the hitting arm toward the spot of contact

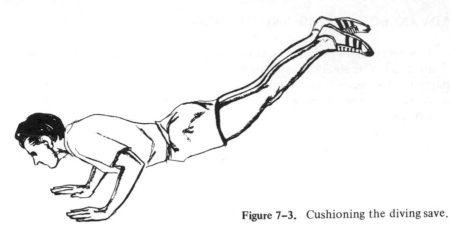

Figure 7–3. Cushioning the diving save.

with the fist clenched and with the back of the hand toward the floor. Turn the side of the body somewhat under you, with a slight stomach-down position. Watch the ball until you have made contact with it on either the fist, wrist, or forearm, and then immediately tuck your head to your chest in preparation for a shoulder-roll landing. At the same time, prepare to absorb part of the shock of landing on your hand and forearm and tuck your shoulder (of the hitting hand) under so that you may then land on the back of that shoulder. Allow your hips and legs to continue on over your landing point, thereby executing a normal shoulder roll. Figure 7–4 shows the correct takeoff position, contact with the ball, first contact with the mat with the off hand (that not used in hitting the ball) and forearm, and the rolling landing.

Practice this maneuver on a mat without a ball until you have the landing well under control. While still on the mat, have someone toss a ball just out of normal side reach and practice the skill with a ball. Finally, move off the mat and practice the skill without and then with a ball.

TABLE 7–4   Common Faults and Corrections — Diving Saves

COMMON FAULT	PROBABLE RESULT	CORRECTION
Diving at a ball within normal reach	Loss of normal control of pass	Don't leave your feet unless necessary to save a ball
Failing to slide or roll after contact with floor	Jarring landing — possible injury	Do not attempt to catch yourself, but distribute the force by sliding or rolling
Failure to watch the ball until contact	Ball is missed altogether or poorly played	Watch the ball strike your hand or wrist
Failure to anticipate need to leave the feet to make a save	Late in getting to the ball	You must have your center of gravity moving toward the ball before you leave your feet

Figure 7–4. Diving save and shoulder-roll recovery.

The Sprawl

One of the newer techniques developed by and for advanced players is a defensive maneuver called the sprawl. This technique is used by a stationary defensive player when the ball is directed into his defensive area and time does not permit the use of a routine bump or dig, and the proximity of the ball to the floor does not leave sufficient time for forward momentum toward the ball before the dive can be executed. The sprawl may be utilized from a basic ready position without forward momentum being established.

The sprawl is executed by a defensive player in the ready position with a right-foot-forward staggered stance and a low center of gravity (Figure 7–5). As the player sees the ball's descent and realizes the ball will land several feet ahead, the player initiates the necessary action by pushing off with both feet and dropping his or her left knee and hand to the floor. At the same time, the player lunges, upper body forward, with the right arm and hand extended toward the ball, parallel and very close to the playing surface. As the body reaches a fully extended position with the palm down and right arm extended forward as far as possible, the ball is contacted with the back of the hand and given additional momentum with an upward flick of the wrist if necessary. The player then absorbs the shock of the contact with the ground with the right hand and forearm and completes the sprawling action on the floor. When the ball continues in play, the alert player must scramble back to a ready position to continue play whether the team is on offense or defense.

Inverted Bump

One of the most difficult reception areas in terms of ball placement and body position is that of a ball traveling in level flight that must be played between chest and head height. Many women players have developed a logical method of playing such a ball, and the technique is finally being used by accomplished male players also. The technique now used by players of both sexes is called an inverted bump pass. It is assumed when using the inverted bump skill that the ball is coming directly at a player with sufficient speed and height to rule out the normal above-the-face pass or the normal underhand, straight-armed dig. Figure 7–6 shows a player utilizing the inverted bump pass on a ball at slightly above chest height.

Inverted-bump skill

When you are unable to play the ball by the normal bump method because of its trajectory and speed, clasp your hands together in the manner normally used for the bump pass. Bend the elbows to a maximum angle, with the hands together, little-finger side of the hand to the front. The ball is contacted with the outside edges of the hands or the wrists, depending on the final height at which the ball is played. To check the correct arm position, assume the normal

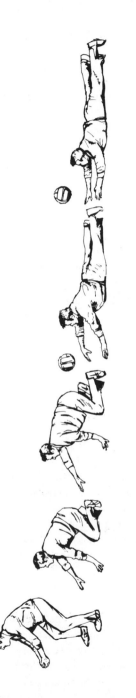

Figure 7–5. The sprawl.

Figure 7–6. Inverted-bump pass.

bumping position and then, without detaching the hands, bend the elbows and rotate the hands and forearms to a position in front of the face.

ADVANCED SPIKING SKILLS

The heart of the ability of the offense to put the ball "on the floor" lies in the ability of individual spikers to successfully attack a ball set in the spiking zone. Beginning players with enough jumping ability and coordination to succeed in early efforts to produce a hard-hit spike see little need to develop alternative skills. But as the capability of the block and defensive team increases, it becomes apparent that a player must be able to do more with a set than pound away at the ball time after time. Efforts at completing a successful attack (putting the ball away) on a set into the spiking zone, with methods other than a hard-driven spike, are divided into three general categories: (1) dink shots, (2) change of pace spikes, and (3) change of direction shots. The latter of these methods actually involves a discussion of defensive positions and blocking patterns, which was presented in the previous chapter.

The Dink Shot

One of the methods of attempting to put the ball on the floor, by means other than a hard-driven spike, involves a very softly played lob shot called a dink. The placement and correct usage of the dink shot depend a great deal on the ability of the defensive team members to block and on their ability to cover the court. By studying the positioning of an opposing team, a spiker may determine one or more desirable areas of placement for the dink shot. Generally

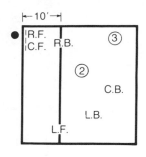

Figure 7-7. Court areas for the dink shot, back-up player (R.B.) close.

speaking, the court areas left unguarded by normal defensive alignment are: (1) the area directly behind the block, (2) the area in front of the front-line player not involved in the block, and (3) an area deep and to either corner. Figures 7-7 and 7-8 designate these areas on a defensive court displaying a typical defensive alignment. The areas are numbered in order of usual preference for shot placement.

Dink skill

The most important aspect of completing a successful dink shot is to mask your intent until the actual moment of contact. You must learn to jump as high as possible using the same jumping technique you employ on a spike. Figure 7-9 shows proper contact for the dink shot. At the last moment, you stiffen the wrist of the spiking hand and extend the fingers toward the ball. The ball itself is actually struck with the finger tips or semifist in a soft, almost pushing motion. The wrist remains stiff throughout the motion, and the slight amount of force needed for the shot comes from upper arm extension from the elbow. Some players are able to use a semifist on the ball and achieve the same effect. You should attempt both types of contact to try to achieve the dinking style best for you. In using either method of striking the ball, however, strive to have the ball travel to the desired court area with a minimum of height in order to minimize the efforts of the defensive team to reach the ball.

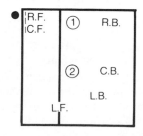

Figure 7-8. Court areas for the dink shot, back-up player (R.B.) deep.

Figure 7–9. Dink shot.

Change-of-Pace Spikes

The actual use of variations in the height of the set accounts for a large portion of the attempts by the spiking team to change the pace of the attack. A normal set will attain a height of 15 feet or more above the net, and while this height gives the spiker adequate time to approach, jump, and complete the spike, it also gives the defensive team adequate time to form and execute a good block. Well drilled offensive teams resort to several different types of spikes in attempting to throw the defense off balance. The three most frequently used change of ·

TABLE 7-5 Common Faults in the Dink Shot and Corrections

COMMON FAULT	PROBABLE RESULT	CORRECTION
Failure to hit the ball softly	Ball travels in high arc — defensive team easily gets to the ball	Work for a true "soft" lob shot — take almost all force away
Telegraphing the intent of the play	Defensive team able to "read the shot" and react	Mask the coming soft hit until the last possible moment
Consistent overuse of the dink shot	Opponents anticipate the dink and react to it	Don't fall into a consistent pattern of play — mix them up — the dink shot is most effective following several hard-driven spikes
Throwing the ball with a wrist motion	Referee calls a foul for "throwing" the ball	Keep a stiff wrist — don't "break" the wrist

pace spikes are: the "shoot" set, the "quickie" set, and the off-speed hit of a regular set.

The shoot set

The shoot set is actually a prearranged play between the setter and the spiker, and usually called by the setter. When the shoot set is called, the setter will attempt to set the ball in a low-line drive at a height some 3 to 4 feet above the net when it crosses the net boundary line (tape). The ball is also set fairly close to the net in addition to traveling in a flat arc parallel to the net.

Shoot-Set Spiking Skill. The primary emphasis in learning to spike the shoot set is placed on correct timing. You must have confidence in your setter and expect the ball to be in the proper position at the net when the shoot set has been called. Your approach should be similar to the regular approach, except

TABLE 7-6 Common Faults in Spiking the Shoot Set and Corrections

COMMON FAULT	PROBABLE RESULT	CORRECTION
Taking off too early	Ball will be hit with lack of power — possibly into the net	Take off as the setter touches the ball
Attempting to hit down the line	Ball is hit out of bounds or directly into the block	Attempt to hit the shoot set on a cross-court angle
Taking off too late	Ball is already past the spiking zone when it is hit — spiker is called for; a carry or a "save" is required	Be in the air in position to spike the ball when it arrives
Attempting to hit a poorly placed shoot set with power	Ball is hit out of bounds or in the net	If a called shoot set is poorly delivered, make every effort to keep it in play — "save it"

that you start toward the net before you actually know exactly where the ball will be. Your actual takeoff occurs at the approximate time the setter is releasing the ball. This timing is quicker than normal and requires a well placed set in order to be effective. You normally attempt to spike the ball cross court, over the middle blocker, in an attempt to beat the block or at least catch the second blocker arriving at the block late. The experienced player will recognize the necessity for simply keeping the ball in play if the set deviates markedly from the expected position. For this reason the shoot set is generally called for only when the pass to the setter is in perfect position. Even then, constant practice in hitting the shoot set is required if consistency is to be gained.

The quickie

Experience in international competition has added a fairly new dimension in spiking tactics. Observation of the Japanese national teams has led to the development of the very short, quick set and spike known as the Japanese set or quick set. Again this spike is actually a prearranged play involving the setter and spiker and demands a maximum of split second timing and knowledge of individual abilities as well as constant practice. When the setter calls a quick set, he or she will attempt to set the ball just above the top of the net and no more than 1 foot back from the net. Figure 7–10 shows the set and spike of a quickie.

Quickie Set Spiking Skill. Timing on the quick set is vital. You must learn to time your approach, jump, and arm swing to arrive at a point just above the setter's outstretched hands as the set is released. Frequently the ball should be spiked on its way up. The quick set is not hit with the all-out power of a normal spike, but is regarded as a finesse shot. Your ability to time the shot and place it in an unguarded court area will determine the effectiveness of the play. If the set is poorly delivered, make every effort to keep the ball in play by simply getting the ball over the net in some legal manner. The common faults and corrections for the quick set are much the same as those for the shoot set.

The off-speed spike

Most basic defensive alignments are designed to stop the hard-driven spikes; secondary emphasis is placed on the coverage of the dink shot. As the ball is spiked, players on the defensive team are moving into designated positions on the floor, usually in a low crouching stance. The off-speed spike is designed to change the timing of the defense players and to bring about possible errors or weak returns.

Off-Speed Spiking Skill. There is actually little difference between the normal spiking action and the action on the off-speed spike. Your arm action is simply less vigorous, resulting in less power behind the ball, and your angle of attack is changed from a sharp downward direction to a looping, deeper point of attack. You must take care to emphasize the amount of overspin placed on the ball in order that the ball will descend into the opponents' court rather than

Figure 7–10. The quickie set.

going out of bounds. To place more overspin on the ball, loosen up your wrist and exaggerate your follow-through. Attempt to hit the ball over the block and deep into the opponents' court.

IMPROVING THE NORMAL ATTACK

Players who normally assume the role of the spiker during competition should constantly seek ways through which the normal spike may become more effective. One frequently neglected method lies in the improvement of the body mechanics used in the jump and preparatory movements before the ball is actually spiked. The jump itself may be improved through the training procedures described in Chapter 3. Also, many players have found that the height of the jump may be increased by utilizing an exaggerated squatting position as a preliminary movement to the actual takeoff for the jump. During the takeoff, both of your arms should thrust violently upward to full extension with the thrusting action actually instigating the jumping action. As soon as your feet leave the ground, you must begin to assume the hitting position offering the greatest summation of forces at the moment of contact with the ball. This position may be described as an "inverted-C" position of the upper and lower body. Figure 4–21, illustrating proper spiking action, shows the correct alignment of the head, shoulders, arms, and legs. Note that in the first illustration in the spiking sequence, the upper body has been hyperextended from the normal vertical plane in order to place the hitting hand and arm as far as possible from the intended point of contact with the ball. In the same illustration, the upper legs have also been drawn back from the vertical plane, and the lower legs, from the knees down, have been drawn up to a horizontal position. As the spiker prepares to make contact with the ball (initiate the forward swing of the hitting arm), the upper body and legs begin to be drawn back toward the vertical plane, as shown in the second, third, and fourth examples in Figure 4–21. As the ball is actually spiked, the body is in a nearly normal vertical plane (example 3). The follow-through carries the upper body and legs to a normal-C position. It should also be noted that in order for the inverted-C position to be assumed, the abdomen and hips have been extended forward as far as possible, and when the reversing action takes place so that the normal-C position is reached, the hips and abdomen have been drawn back past the normal vertical plane.

A second method of bringing about overall improvement in spiking may be found in the process of learning and using the angle shots available to the spiker. With the present trend toward the use of multiple offensive patterns, each player should learn to spike the ball away from a one- or two-player block and still keep the ball in the court. When spiking from the left-front court position, if you find the block to the inside of the court, and the ball is set somewhere near the side line, the ball should be spiked "down the line," or at an almost perpendicular angle to the net. Conversely, if the block is formed near the side line, you may wish to spike the ball at an angle more toward the center of the opponents' court, or "inside the block." In both instances, if the ball is struck with full power, the necessary adjustment in the swing must be accomplished at the start of the forward motion of the arm. If the ball is to be struck down the line, the nonhitting shoulder is drawn slightly back in order to bring the shoulders parallel to the net so that the hitting arm may be brought forward in a line perpendicular to the net. If the ball is to be "cut" (or hit on the inside angle), the nonhitting shoulder is drawn forward and down toward the midline of the body, thereby raising the hitting shoulder slightly, and allowing the hitting arm to be brought through on an inside-to-outside line. Very advanced spikers work on delaying these preliminary shoulder movements until the last possible second, in order to reduce the time available to the defense to react in the direction of the flight of the spiked ball.

It should be emphasized that the skills described in this chapter are advanced skills and demand perfection of technique and understanding of overall strategy before they are effective. The casual participant in power volleyball should be able to enjoy the game by a mastery of fundamentals. It is not necessary to learn and practice these advanced skills.

8□Evaluation

As is the case with many participants in team games, beginning volleyball players soon seek to determine how their individual skills and knowledge level are progressing. Most players are somewhat aware of their overall contribution to the effort of the team, but still desire to ascertain the strengths and weaknesses that are present in individuals. They become aware that power volleyball is a game of many intricate skills, such as serving, receiving, spiking, setting, and blocking. The ability to develop these skills depends on many separate physical characteristics, such as timing, agility, strength, and the ability to react rapidly to certain stimuli. Still further, the players beyond the very beginning level recognize that despite adequate or superior physical attributes and properly developed skills, it is necessary to have a basic knowledge of the game before the physical abilities and skills can be put to good use. All too often a player with superior physical abilities and perhaps above-average height develops one or two skills (such as spiking and blocking) to an advanced level and neglects most of the other facets of the game. When viewed from a subjective standpoint, this player is seemingly a very advanced player and makes a significant contribution to a team's effort. But when evaluated objectively in several skills, overall physical abilities, and knowledge of the game, his weaknesses and detrimental effect on overall team effort are apparent.

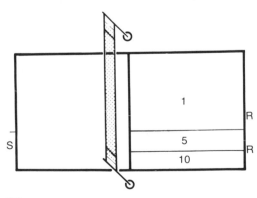

Figure 8–1. Diagram for serving tests. Equipment needed: one or two volleyballs for each court and masking tape.

SKILL TESTS

At the present time there is a very real lack of tests in certain skill areas, such as spiking and blocking, as well as a lack of skill tests to evaluate advanced players. Skill tests may be used, however, to test serving, passing, bump passing, set-up placement, and retrieving the ball from the net. In all instances skill tests have been selected that demand a minimum of equipment and preparation and provide simple scoring methods.

Serving Tests

The serve may be executed by either the underhand or the overhead method, depending on the age and skill level of the participants. The server stands behind the end line, within 10 feet of the right side line. Figure 8–1 shows the proper court markings for the serve test. The court opposite the server is marked by masking tape into three areas. These areas extend the full 30-foot length of the court and are 4-feet, 6-feet, and 20-feet wide. The server is allowed 10 trials, attempting to place each serve over the net and as close to the 4-foot area (area 10 on the diagram) as possible. The 4-foot lane counts 10 points, the adjacent 6-foot lane (area 5 on the diagram) counts five points and the remaining 20-foot wide zone (marked 1 on the diagram) counts one point. A ball that contacts the net or travels out of bounds, either long or wide, counts as a trial but receives no score. A ball landing on a line receives the highest of the possible scores. A total of 100 points is possible. The diagram also shows the position of two retrievers stationed behind the back line of the scoring zones, one of whom is required to keep track of the number of trials remaining; the other records the points scored.

Advanced players wishing to evaluate serving skill are required to undergo self-evaluation based on several factors related to actual game conditions. A subjective evaluation should be based on the overall consistency with which the serve is delivered into the opponents' court in a legal manner, as well as the action of the ball. A well delivered punch serve should have sufficient force to bring about the desired "knuckle ball" effect and yet maintain the desired placement. The overhead power serve and the roundhouse serve should be delivered with sufficient power to enable the ball to dip into the court with considerable force.

TABLE 8–1 Norms for the Serving Test

	AVERAGE	GOOD	EXCELLENT
Women	30–49	50–69	70–100
Men	45–69	70–84	85–100

Passing Tests

Beginners may be tested in their ability to execute the above-the-face pass by
the use of a wall-volley test. This test is a very simple one and should be used to
determine whether beginning players have developed the minimum skills necessary to execute the basic pass. The test may be conducted against any unob-
structed wall surface and lines necessary may be constructed with masking tape.
A player stands behind a 6-foot restraining line parallel to the test wall and is
timed for 30 seconds on his ability to pass the ball repeatedly above the 10-foot
line on the test wall. Upon the starting signal, the player tosses the ball against
the wall and then volleys the return until stopped by the time limit or until the
ball is misplayed (returned under the 10-foot height, thrown, fails to reach the
wall, and so forth). When the ball is misplayed, the player retosses the ball and
begins the process from that return. The total number of volleys touching the
wall on or above the 10-foot line, multiplied by three, constitutes the overall
score for each player.

Set-up Tests

Tests used to determine the set-up ability of a player should be recognized as
slightly advanced tests for the basic above-the-face pass. In order for beginning
players to be tested on set-up ability, each player must have a minimum skill
level in the basic pass. Set-up tests differ from wall-volley tests in that they
emphasize accuracy and height of the pass rather than rapidity. Figure 8–2
and the accompanying table show a court prepared for the set-up test, norms for
men and women, and equipment needed. A second pair of net standards are
placed approximately 10 feet apart, 8 feet from a normally rigged net at mid-
court. A rope or string is attached to the extra standards at a height of 8 feet
from the floor to form a barrier parallel to the net, 8 feet from the net and 8
feet high. The player taking the test (marked X on the diagram) stands an additional 8 feet back from the barrier, or a total of 16 feet from the net. As he
receives a ball tossed in the air by a second player (marked T) slightly in front
and to the right of the player taking the test, he attempts to set the ball over the
barrier so that it lands as close as possible to the target areas marked on the floor
at the middle of the court. The target areas are two concentric half circles with a
radius of 2 feet and 6 feet, extending toward the player from the center line. A
ball hitting the smaller of the two circles is given a score of 10 points, and a ball
landing in the larger of the two areas but outside the middle area is scored as five
points. A ball traveling over the barrier but failing to land in the target area is
given two points. Any ball failing to clear the 8-foot barrier, landing over the
net, or contacting the net is scored 0. Ten trials are given and the total score
possible is 100. If the ball is erratically tossed to the player taking the test, he
or she may catch the ball and return it to the tosser without having it count as
one of the 10 allowable trials. If the player attempts to set the ball, even if not
perfectly thrown, it counts as a trial.

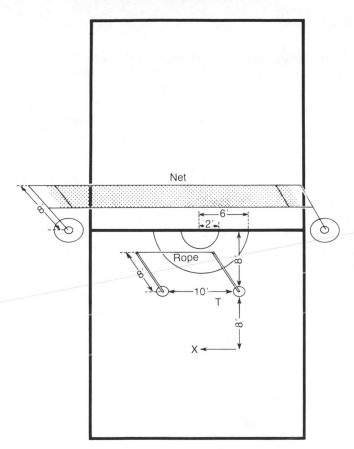

Figure 8–2. Diagram for set-up tests. Equipment needed: two extra volleyball standards, 10-foot rope or heavy twine, volleyballs, magic marker, and normal volleyball court and net.

TABLE 8–2   Norms for Set-up Test

	AVERAGE	GOOD	EXCELLENT
Women	30–44	45–59	60–100
Men	40–54	55–69	70–100

Advanced players may again be forced to rely on self-evaluation to determine set-up skill. A frequently used method is to stand on the free throw line of a basketball court and attempt to set the ball through the basket. Skilled players should be consistently able to make the ball contact the rim before striking the backboard, even if the ball fails to go through the basket. The same technique may be used to evaluate over-the-head passing ability by simply turning so that the back is toward the goal and repeating the same procedures.

Bump Pass

The forearm-bump pass is tested by much the same procedure as the wall-volleyball test. The same flat wall surface used for the wall volley may be utilized except that no marking on the wall is required. The 6-foot restraining line is still maintained, however. The player taking the test stands behind the restraining line facing the wall. As the start command is given, he tosses the ball in an underhand motion against the wall and attempts to bump the ball repeatedly against the wall without misplaying the ball. If the ball is misplayed (e.g., played with the hands open, double hit, fails to reach the walls, touches the floor), the player retrieves the ball and retosses it against the wall in order to resume scoring. Each legal bump pass contacting the wall from a starting position behind the restraining line counts three points. If the player steps over the line as he bumps, the bump does not count, but it is not necessary to retoss the ball before legal bumps may be counted again. The total score is the number of legal bumps contacting the wall in 30 seconds. Table 8–3 shows norms for the bump pass for men and women.

TABLE 8–3   Norms for Bump-Pass Test

	POOR	AVERAGE	GOOD	EXCELLENT
Women	Up to 17	18–27	28–34	35 +
Men	Up to 21	22–31	32–39	40 +

Advanced players attempt to combine bump-pass accuracy and height control and above-the-face pass accuracy and height control by using a self-evaluation technique involving both skills. Standing in the middle of a circle approximately 12 feet in diameter (basketball free-throw circle), the player sets the ball to herself and then bumps the set into the air directly over her head. She then proceeds to alternate bump passes and above-the-face passes without having to leave the circle or restart the drill. Advanced players should be able to keep the ball in motion for a considerable length of time using only legal passing techniques. A variation of this drill for very advanced players has the player contact the ball only by the above-the-face pass but alternates passing from a sitting and standing position. This drill requires and demonstrates extreme passing accuracy and agility.

Net Retrieving

The skill of retrieving the ball from the net is a difficult one and requires a certain amount of judgment. An assistant tosses the ball into the net at various heights and speeds, and the player attempts to play the ball on the rebound from the net. Scoring is based on the total points scored in 10 trials, with a ball retrieved from the net and played into the opponents' court counting 10 points; a ball staying on the offensive side of the net but played high enough to be kept in play counting five points; and a ball misplayed or illegally played counting 0. It must be emphasized that to be legally played, the ball must be played with the closed fist or fists or the back of the hand.

Spiking Test

Attempts thus far to evaluate spiking skill objectively have proved to be fairly unreliable. Since spiking is such an important part of the game of power volleyball, some method of evaluation is usually attempted on a subjective basis. This evaluation should be based on several factors, however, and should be considered on the basis of more than one attempt. A skillful setter should be used for all the players being evaluated, or if sufficient setting skill is lacking, an assistant should be utilized to toss the ball in an underhand motion to a point 12 to 15 feet above the net with some degree of consistency for each trial. The points that should be considered by the evaluation (or during self-evaluation) are:

1. The downward angle of the ball into the opponents' court
2. The technique used to attempt to produce overspin on the ball
3. The speed generated on the spike
4. The placement of the spike (possibly predetermined by the tester, e.g., down the line, deep, cross court)
5. Total legality of the attempt

IMPORTANT PHYSICAL CHARACTERISTICS

In many instances it becomes desirable to attempt to identify the specific kinetic and physical attributes that are present in outstanding performers in a sport. These factors may be found to be important in evaluation or in team selection. A recent study done in the area of power volleyball attempted to identify these attributes in volleyball players. Although there were many items tested in comparing beginning college players and volleyball participants of Olympic caliber, only a few items were found to be of real importance in discerning a difference in the players. The physical abilities that were found to be superior in the top players included vertical jumping ability, reaction time, grip strength, and the ability to move rapidly in a lateral direction. The only physical characteristic that was found to be superior was height.

It would seem that if test items other than skill tests were to be used, an attempt would be made to evaluate those characteristics that are easily measured and require little equipment. Such items as height, vertical jumping ability, and agility seem to fall into this category. Although height and vertical jumping

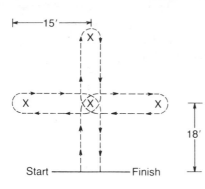

Figure 8–3. Diagram for agility run.

ability may be accurately measured in a variety of ways, the need for a good test of agility is apparent. McCloy and Young* have described a test for agility involving a cloverleaf run that has fairly high reliability and validity. The agility run may be conducted with no more equipment than a stopwatch, four small movable objects (paper cups, Indian clubs, for example), and normal gymnasium floor space. Each player should be allowed to become familiar with the course to be followed and then allowed two trials, the better of the two attempts being recorded. Figure 8–3 illustrates the course to be followed and Table 8–4, the norms for men and women. The distance between the start-finish line and the center object is 18 feet, and the distance between the center object and each of the three remaining points is 15 feet. Note that each participant should always return to the center and turn right before continuing to the next point in the course.

TABLE 8–4 Norms for Agility Run

	POOR	AVERAGE	GOOD	EXCELLENT
Women	12.5 sec. and above	12.4 to 11.4	11.3 to 10.5	10.4 and below
Men	12.0 sec. and above	11.9 to 11.0	10.9 to 10.0	9.9 and below

*C. H. McCloy and Norma D. Young: Tests and Measurements in Physical Education. New York: Appleton-Century-Crofts, Inc., Publishers, 1954, p. 77.

9 □ Individual and Team Practice Hints

Understanding of rules, strategy, and court position and knowledge of skill mechanics are necessary in order for the beginning player of power volleyball to feel at home on the courts. But most players soon reach the logical point of wishing to improve their own individual skills in order to better enjoy game competition. In many class or team practice sessions it is possible for individual players to become more competent by simply taking part in normal play involving full teams of six players on a side. However, it is also possible that an individual will make time for practice when classes or teams are not scheduled to meet. Almost all the skills necessary in power volleyball can be practiced individually or with one or two additional players, as long as minimum floor space and equipment are available.

As in any sport, consistent and well structured practice sessions are a must for improvement, and individual players desiring to become more competent in volleyball must be willing to devote time to nonteam or nonclass organizational settings. A player who is weak in a given skill should be willing to work or practice on that skill until it is at least on a level with his remaining skills. Conversely, a player who is very skilled in one phase of the game may wish to work on that particular skill in order to become an outstanding and consistent point-winner because of his excellence in that skill. This emphasis on a single skill is desirable only if a player is able to maintain reasonably broad competence in the remaining skills. The following discussion concerning practice hints for individuals or groups of two, three, or four players is based on the assumption that at least one volleyball and minimal floor space are available.

INDIVIDUAL DRILLS

One-Player Drills

Any individual player is able to work extensively on volleyball skills provided he or she understands the mechanics of the skill and is able to evaluate progress, at least in a subjective manner. The amount of benefit to the player working alone is limited only by the individual's imagination, perseverance, and willingness to spend sufficient time to actually achieve excellence.

Wall spike

Once you understand the fundamental movements in the spiking action, you must be willing to practice alone on those mechanics until they are mastered. In the wall-spiking drill you should stand with a regulation volleyball at a 15- to 18-foot distance from a flat, fairly high wall surface. Toss the ball into the air slightly in front of your spiking arm and spike the ball at the floor a few feet from the wall. If the ball is struck properly, it will rebound from the floor to the wall and then back to you at a height sufficiently high to be spiked again. With some practice you should be able to regulate the force with which the ball is struck to the point that the ball returns to you in a controlled arc at the approximate point where it was originally spiked. As you become proficient at this drill, you may wish to add a normal two-footed takeoff to your spiking technique. Even very advanced players resort to this drill to ensure correct arm action and to warm up before attempting spiking effort in a practice or match session.

Pass to self

Stand in the middle of a predetermined floor area (e.g., basketball free-throw circle, one half of a badminton court) and toss the ball above your head 6 to 8 feet. Move rapidly under the ball and, utilizing an above-the-face pass, set the ball fairly high into the air, attempting to keep the ball's downward flight within the predetermined floor space. Again move rapidly under the ball, making sure that your feet are set and that you are using correct passing mechanics, and continue to pass the ball to yourself with a minimum of foot movement.

Bump pass

Once you have mastered the pass-to-self practice drill, you should attempt to incorporate a bump pass into the drill by bumping the ball straight up on alternating passes. As you are learning the drill, it is permissible, and possibly even necessary, to utilize two successive bump passes in order to keep the ball in the air. Strive to achieve smooth controlled above-the-face passes and high controlled bump passes. It is important to remember that utilization of correct techniques in both the above-the-face pass and the bump pass is more important to overall improvement than resorting to illegal or poor techniques simply to keep the ball in the air or contained in the specified floor area.

Wall-serve bump

If you are able to utilize any type of flat wall surface, you should attempt to perfect your serving techniques as well as improve your ability to bump a ball coming to you in a horizontal manner. Stand facing the wall at a distance of 15 to 20 feet from the junction of the floor and wall. Serve to a point on the wall approximately 9 feet from the floor. This height may be estimated or predetermined by measurement and marked with a short strip of removable masking tape. By a short period of experimentation you should be able to determine the correct serving force to ensure a rebound from the wall into the approximate location where you may attempt a bump pass. In performing this drill, emphasis should be placed on serving the ball in the correct manner for the type of serve you are attempting and in utilizing correct mechanics for the execution of the bump pass.

As you perfect the skills involved in this drill, you should also try to ensure that the ball rebounding from the wall on the serve is bumped high in the air so that the descent of the ball brings it to a point directly in front of you at a distance of 4 to 6 feet from the wall. A helpful technique in bringing about this control is to assume the straight-armed, thumbs-pointing-toward-the-ground, bumping technique immediately after serving the ball. The knees should also be flexed as you wait for the ball before attempting the bump.

Block over the net

In this simple blocking drill you should attempt to stand close to the net and jump as high as possible, reaching as far over the net as possible without contacting the net in any manner. Be sure that after jumping and reaching you land on your side of the center line and regain your balance without stepping over the center line.

A variation of the same drill should be used to perfect the technique of moving three or four steps laterally as rapidly as possible followed by a maximum effort to make a blocking jump. Practice moving from the middle of the net to a position at the intersection of the side line and the net before you attempt to jump. You will also find that you are able to move slightly faster in a lateral direction if your first step is a small cross-over as opposed to the traditional elongated step taken by the lead foot.

Two-Player Drills

Much valuable practice may be accomplished by two players if they utilize practice time in performing actual skill improvement drills. Many of the practice drills are also used extensively as warm-up activity by all members of a team before a competitive match. A player who is able to control the flight of the ball successfully in the variety of two-player drills that follows will usually have an advantage in performing the necessary skills during actual game conditions.

Pass drill

While it is possible for you to practice the above-the-face pass to some extent by yourself, in order to simulate normal game conditions, you should spend as much time as possible in a simple two-person passing drill. You should face your partner at a distance of 6 to 10 feet and attempt to pass the ball in a controlled arc so that the path of the ball's vertical descent is located directly over your partner's head. The height of the ball should be regulated by the distance separating the two players. The farther apart you are as the ball is passed, the higher the arc of the ball. Advanced players can gain valuable "touch" or feeling for the pass by allowing the path of the ball to become almost horizontal between partners. When you first attempt this particular variation, remember that in order to be effective the ball must be kept above shoulder height. Another reminder to be considered by both beginning and advanced players is that the person to whom you are passing the ball will have much more success in controlling the ball if he or she is allowed to step forward or remain stationary in order to play the ball, rather than being forced to step backward to do so.

Spike-dig drill

This is a drill used almost universally by players in a competitive training session, in a twofold attempt to learn to control the direction and downward angle of a spike, and in an effort to dig or bump a spiked ball. Stand 15 to 20 feet from your partner and throw the ball in an arc that will bring the ball down near his or her standing position. Your partner will spike the ball at you, directing the ball to a point directly in front of you at about knee height. You in turn should bump the ball in a controlled arc so that it descends in such a manner that it may be respiked and the drill continued.

Correct arm action is a must in controlling the spike and imparting the desired amount of overspin to the ball. Practice in controlling the amount of force delivered to the spike, dependent on the distance separating the two players, will give the bumping partner an opportunity to play the ball correctly, as well as giving the spiking partner valuable experience in spike placement. In the event that the ball is spiked to either side rather than directly in front of you, attempt to bump the ball normally by turning to the side and utilizing both arms. If, however, the ball is out of reach when using both arms, resort to a one-armed dig, remembering that the fist must be kept clenched during the digging action.

This drill should be a part of every practice session, with partners alternating spiking and digging or bumping after several separate repetitions. As experience is gained in the drill, you may find it possible to move a greater distance apart in order that the ball may be spiked with considerable force, actually approximating the spiking speed found in actual play. At a greater distance and thus greater speed, you are also able to gain valuable experience in "reading" the direction of the spike before it is actually struck. Watch the arm and upper body of the spiker and you will note that it is possible to anticipate the angle and direction of the spike by observing movements of body segments as the player prepares to strike the ball. This "reading" of placement of a spike is somewhat easier when the spiker actually leaps in the air under normal spiking conditions. You should also be able to determine that a dink or soft spike is forthcoming by the preliminary arm action of the spiker.

Dive-roll drill

When you reach the point that you are ready to attempt to increase your horizontal playing area, you must spend extensive practice in a drill utilizing the dive-and-roll technique described in Chapter 7. A partner with a volleyball should stand facing you at a distance of 8 to 10 feet. The ball should be thrown to either side just beyond your normal reaching ability. You should attempt to leave your feet, contact the ball while in mid-air, and land in the correct rolling maneuver in order to regain your feet, ready to play the ball again. You will find that if the person tossing the ball understands your capabilities, he or she can gradually increase the distance to the side at which the ball is thrown, effecting a considerable increase in your lateral coverage.

The same type of drill may be utilized to increase your ability to move forward to reach the ball, the forward dive-and-slide being utilized rather than the rolling recovery. In either case it is important that you practice both the dive and the recovery on a mat without the ball and then on a mat with the ball before moving to the regular floor surface. Keep in mind that these drills emphasize *saving* tactics and that normal passing mechanics should be used whenever possible.

No-spike game at the net

When players are able to utilize a net in their practice efforts, a no-spike game may be used to increase touch and mobility on the court. Face your partner across the net, with each player 3 to 5 feet from the net. Pass the ball just over the net, attempting to place the ball as close to the opposite side of the net as possible. Your partner should attempt to return the ball using either a pass or a bump, keeping the ball low and as close to your side of the net as possible. Do not allow the ball to stray markedly in a lateral direction, and restart the drill whenever the ball is misplayed or placed beyond the reach of either player. No spiking is allowed and only legal bumps and passes should be used. Once the game is under way, you will find that, if you are able to place the ball so that it actually touches the top of the net as it travels over the net, the path of the ball will be altered, forcing your partner to adjust his or her attempts to play the ball. Valuable experience in playing the ball from the net may also be gained in using this particular drill.

Blocking drill

By working in pairs, two players may use a simple blocking and moving drill that will enable these skills to be improved for actual game conditions. Face your partner on the opposite side of the net while standing on one side of the court near the intersection of net and side line. On the go signal, leap straight up in the air as high as possible and make contact with both your partner's hands. Land legally on your side of the net and take three slide-steps toward the middle of the net while your partner does the same. At the end of the third step gather yourself for a second leap, again attempting to contact both hands of your partner above the net. Upon landing, take three more slide-steps, bringing you to a position near the intersection of the net and side line across the court from your original position. From this position, again leap and make contact with your partner above the plane of the net. Make sure you do not contact the net in any manner during the blocking attempts or during the sliding movement. By watching your partner you will soon develop the proper rhythm to enable you to time your jumps and steps so that you both arrive at the correct jumping position at the same time.

Three-Player Drills

Although it is possible that three players may be forced to practice together with no additional players present, it is more likely that groups of three players may combine to utilize the specific drills designed to include that number. Many of the drills presented for two players may be expanded to include three players, but the two new drills presented here are specific in their attempt to utilize three players.

Back-set drill

One of the advanced skills that should be practiced regularly is the skill of passing the ball over the head to a player positioned behind the passer. In order to facilitate this pass, stand midway between two players, who are facing each other about 20 feet apart. The drill should be started by the player you are facing, who will pass the ball fairly high in the air so that its downward trajectory places it near your position. Move directly under the ball and attempt to set the ball high in the air to the third player located behind you, using correct behind-the-back setting mechanics. You must be sure that you move almost directly under the ball and contact the ball legally in order to execute the pass. As you gain skill in moving rapidly under the ball, you may wish to turn 180 degrees before the ball arrives and pass the ball in the direction from which it traveled originally. In either case make sure your feet are set and that you are in a balanced position before attempting any behind-the-back pass.

Set-spike-dig drill

With three players it is possible to use a setting, spiking, digging drill that gives each player an opportunity to practice a different skill as each of three positions is attempted. If you start in the setting position, you simply pass the ball from the center of the front line to a spiker who is moving into the spiking zone near the intersection of net and side line. The spiker will attempt to spike the ball directly at the third player in the drill who has positioned himself either in the exact middle of the opposite court or on the side line directly in front of the spiker, at a distance of 20 feet from the net. The person occupying the third, or digging, position should attempt to dig or bump any spiked ball within reach.

After two attempts in the original position, players should rotate to a new position in order to gain experience in that skill. Correct rotation procedure in this drill is for the setter to become the spiker, the spiker to become the digger, and the digger to become the setter. This is an excellent all-purpose drill because it not only includes three distinct skills but allows each of the three players an opportunity to practice skills which may not normally be included in a practice session. Thus, setters may have an opportunity to spike, spikers may take a turn attempting to set the ball, and all players gain experience in back-court play.

Four-Player Drills

It is obvious that if four players have an opportunity to practice together, any number of the drills explained under "Two-Player" and "Three-Player" drills may be used "as is" or altered slightly to include four players. There are, however, two specific activities that four players may engage in somewhat more successfully than smaller groups of players.

Badminton court doubles

A drill used by many players in an attempt to improve ball control and movement on the court utilizes a badminton court and net to replace the standard volleyball court. Serving is restricted to an underhand lob, and no spiking is allowed, of course; otherwise all rules of volleyball are enforced. By using the lowered net and definite court boundaries, both players on each side of the net are forced to move laterally and forward and back in order to satisfactorily cover the court. It should also be noted that no effort is made to utilize all three hits allowed each team. As a result, players are forced to be alert constantly for all types of returns and play possibilities. Each of the four players must reinforce the use of legal mechanics during actual play.

Doubles play

Recognition of the benefit and enjoyment of participation in regulation play involving only two players per team on a normal court has become very widespread. In many areas of the country regular doubles tournaments are held throughout the year, particularly outdoors during the summer months. The practice value of doubles play lies in the fact that when two players are forced to cover a regulation court, each must be able to perform all the normal skills and be able to move rapidly in response to play situations. Corecreational doubles are also used in many areas of the country with the added benefit of social attraction.

Rules for doubles play are identical to six-person play except that games are normally shortened to 11 points and the net height is adjusted to 7 feet 10 inches for men if played on outdoor sand courts. Techniques for participation in doubles play are very similar to techniques for regular team play except that doubles players must also become adept at improvising skills to fit the style of play. In doubles play, for instance, it is quite often desirable to spike the ball as it is bumped on the reception of the serve if the bump places the ball high and near the net or if the bump is high and near mid-court and the opponents are slow to assume correct defensive positions. Also, wise use of the "overset" or ball set in such a manner that it crosses the net into the opponents' court frequently finds the opponents well back in the court anticipating the need to assume a normal defensive, digging stance and position.

When the game is played on sand courts, players must learn to adjust jumping mechanics to eliminate the normal, firmly planted takeoff technique. Also on the sand, players utilize the diving-save technique to a much greater extent because of the favorable landing surface. Players attempting to use doubles play as a method of practice should be sure that each player has a fairly competent range of skills, in order to ensure that a particular weakness on the part of one participant does not hinder the progress of the remaining players.

TEAM PRACTICE HINTS

Although it is not the purpose of this book to discuss team participation or strategy, some thought must be given to the role of the individual's contribution to the overall effectiveness of team practice. Any individual concerned about developing as a player must also be concerned about contributing to a team effort. It has been shown that the success a team enjoys may be directly reflected by the type and organization of regular practice sessions. The effort put forth by all players toward well organized, beneficial practice is an effort that will pay large dividends in team success. The following principles of team practice are usually dependent on cooperation between players and a coach:

1. Place one person in charge of workouts. Frequently when a group of players gather to work on a team basis, no one individual is actually designated as the person in charge of the actual practice. The individual designated should

have the recognized authority (and responsibility) to direct the type and duration of each practice segment.

2. Organize practice into specific time blocks. Every effort should be made to construct practice sessions so that all necessary skills are covered during a given number of practice sessions. The player (or coach) responsible for practice structure should plan the practice in order to include a variety of drills covering as many skills as possible. In certain instances a drill or explanation must be structured to cover only a specific skill or play situation, but when this occurs a specific amount of time should be budgeted for the drill and this time should not be surpassed.

3. Scrimmage alone is not practice. All too often participants in the sport of power volleyball resort to regular intrateam competition as a sole means of practice. There is no doubt that this type of activity is enjoyable and provides a certain amount of improvement in overall skill. It should be noted, however, that game-type scrimmage does not provide any specific structure to work on repetition of weak skill areas, nor does it give team members an opportunity to reinforce court positioning or innovative skill methods. In a well organized team practice session a portion of the total time available may be devoted to game condition scrimmage, but it should not constitute the total practice time.

4. Keep explanations to a minimum. As new team tactics are introduced, care should be taken to ensure that only a minimum amount of verbal explanation is used. Players should be encouraged to give all-out attention to new drills, court coverage, or strategy, as they are explained, in order that a major portion of practice time may be devoted to actual participation in drills or scrimmage. The use of pretyped instruction sheets or short chalk board presentations are both valuable aids in reducing the amount of verbal explanation necessary.

5. Go all-out in drills and scrimmage. One of the more difficult principles for most players to observe is the giving of all-out effort during practice sessions. Many individuals feel that extension of maximum effort should be reserved strictly for game conditions. It is important for every player to attempt to achieve the same type of intense concentration during practice that is normally found in competition.

Players should be made aware that two specific shortcomings are apparent when practice is carried out at submaximum effort. First, in order to coordinate team play among several players, it is necessary to establish a pattern of *timing* on the various play situations. If one player is loafing during the execution of a given offensive play, the other participants in the play are unable to judge accurately the correct sequence of events necessary for successful completion of the play. The setter, for instance, is unable to consistently pass the short pass when different spikers put forth varying amounts of effort in arriving at the net to spike. And finally, each player on the team is able to learn the capabilities of other players during competition only by repeated experience during practice. A player who loafs through practice will discourage teammates from depending on him or her in difficult competition because the ability to make the tough play during practice was not demonstrated.

Glossary

Above-the-face pass — The basic pass in volleyball in which the ball is played from a position directly in front of the face.

Ace serve — Any serve that is delivered in such a manner that the opponents are unable to receive it.

Back-line players — The three player positions behind the front-line players — determined by location at the time of the serve.

Back court spike — An offensive play in which any back-court player attempts to spike the ball from the court area behind the 10-foot spiking line.

Block — An attempt by one or more defensive players to obstruct a hard shot at the net made by the opposing team.

Catch — Allowing the ball to come to rest in any part or parts of the body.

Center back — The player position in the center of the back line.

Center forward — The player position in the center of the front line.

Center line — A line 4 inches wide drawn across the center of the court, directly under the net.

Cover — Players positioning themselves behind a spike or block in order to play a ball glancing off another player.

Cross-court shot — A shot hit from the right or left side of one of the team's court diagonally to the right or left side respectively of the other team's court.

Dead ball — A ball out of play following a point, side out, or any other decision of the referee temporarily suspending play.

Dig — A ball played defensively, usually with one hand, and often used in attempting to play a spiked ball.

Dink shot — A softly played lob shot over the hands of the blockers.

Double hit — A ball hit twice in succession by the same player in a single attempt to play the ball.

End line — A line 2 inches wide parallel to the net and 30 feet from it marking the ends of the court.

Fist ball — A ball struck with the fist, often on a dig.

Flip-flop set — A ball set over the head of the setter to the spiker behind.

Floater — A ball served in such a manner that there is little or no spin imparted to it, causing the ball to weave or float through the air.

Foot fault — Stepping on or over the end line while serving or over the center line during a play at the net.

Foul — Any violation of the general rules of the game.

Four hits — A team foul resulting from the ball being hit four times on one side of the net during a normal play.

Front-line players — The three playing positions at the front of the court that are determined by location at the time of the serve.

Game — The total contest. A game shall end when: (1) either team has scored 15 points with a margin of at least two points, (2) with the score 14–14, play continues until one team has a two-point advantage, or (3) eight minutes of playing time elapse with one team holding a two-point advantage.

Game point — That situation in a game when the serving team is within one point of winning the game.

Half-moon — A semicircular serve reception formation. Also called a crescent formation.

High pass — A ball set unusually high (18 to 22 feet in height) to the spiker so that the spiker will have time to move under the ball before attempting to spike.

In the net — A touching of the net by a player during play. The call "in the net" may be made by either the player himself or an official.

Japanese set — A very short set, usually in the center of the net, given to a spiker who is already in the air and who will attempt to spike the set on the way up.

Jump set — A set made by a player who has jumped off the floor. Usually made by one spiker on the front line attempting to set another spiker in an effort to deceive the opponents.

Kill shot — Any hit in which the ball is hit so sharply or so accurately that the defensive players are not able to return it. Another term for a spike.

Left back — A player position at the left of the back line.

Left front — A player position at the left of the front line.

Liner — A ball that lands on any part of the court boundary lines. It is considered in bounds.

Line officials — Usually two in number, who assist the referee by making decisions on service foot faults and liners. They are positioned diagonally across the court from each other.

Match — The best two out of three or three out of five games.

Net — The basic dividing plane between the two halves of the court. The volleyball net is 36 inches wide and 32 feet long. It is made of cord meshes, 4 inches square. On the top of the net is a canvas band, 2 inches wide.

Net ball — A ball which touches the net.

Net serve — A served ball that touches the net in its flight.

Off-speed spike — A spiked ball that has less than a normal spike speed in an attempt to deceive the opponents.

Out of bounds — A ball is out of bounds when it touches the net outside the net tape or the ground outside the boundary lines.

Out of position — At the start of play (the serve) each player must be in his respective rotation order.

Overlap — A foul committed when an official is not able to determine a player's correct position on the serve. A player may not be incorrectly positioned in relation to the players on either side of him or the player in front or behind him. Overlap is determined by any part of a player's body touching the floor.

Pass — The movement of the ball between teammates. Used in a variety of ways including bump pass, deep pass, above-the-face pass, etc.

Pepper — The two-player drill involving spiking and spike receiving.

Placement serve — A serve which is directed to a spot on the opponents' court which will cause a maximum of difficulty in returning it.

Power serve — A serve in which much momentum is given to the ball by the server who hits the ball with great force, usually in a spiking motion.

Punch serve — A serve struck with a punching motion resulting in little or no spin on the ball. Also called a floater serve.

"Quickie" — A ball that is set to the spiker with considerably less height than a normal set in an attempt to beat the block.

Quick serve — A ball that is served before the receiving team is in position and ready to receive the serve.

Receive — Maneuver used by a player to play a serve.

Referee — The official in charge of the overall conduct of the game, positioned above the net at one end of the net.

Right back — A player position at the right side of the back line.

Right front — A player position at the right side of the front line.

Rotation — The clockwise movement of players on the court after the opponents have lost the serve.

Roundhouse — Action used to strike the ball on a serve or over the net. The ball is struck with the arm fully extended over the head.

Scoop — To lift the ball with the open hands.

Screening — An illegal position taken by two or more players on the serving team in an attempt to screen the ball from the opponents during the serve.

Set — A ball passed into the air near the net by one player so that a teammate can spike the ball sharply downward into the opponents' court.

Setter — Any player executing a set-up pass.

Shoot-set — A type of set in which the ball is played on a low line just above the top of the net and parallel to it.

Spike — A leap into the air and a sharp downward hitting of the ball into the opponents' court.

"Sticky" — A ball that has come to rest in the hands. A ball that is not clearly hit.

Substitution — A player entering the game to replace another player.

Tape — A 2-inch strip of material (tape or canvas) fastened vertically on each side of the net, directly above the side lines, and marking the side boundary lines of the court.

Team — A group of six players on one half of the court.

Throw — A ball that is guided or not clearly hit during play.

Time out — 30-second rest periods during a game.

Umpire — The second in command in the officiating team.

Underhand pass — Hitting the ball with the palms facing upward and the fingers open.

Up — Successful reception of the serve.

Bibliography

Boyden, D., Burton, R. G., and Odeneal, W. T.: *Volleyball Syllabus*. United States Volleyball Association, Berne, Indiana, 1969. (A useful syllabus presenting many aspects of the game as well as information on officials, tournament planning, and clinic presentations.)

Keller, V.: *Point, Game, and Match!* Creative Sports Books, Hollywood, California, 1968. (Comprehensive book intended for advanced players, with good sections on coaching techniques and practice organization.)

LaVeaga, R.: *Volleyball*. Ronald Press Co., New York, 1960. (A general coverage of several aspects of the game, intended for the basic beginner.)

Marshall, S. H.: *Capsule History of Volleyball*. Creative Sports Books, Hollywood, California, 1968. (Coverage of the rapid rise of volleyball to an Olympic sport, including scores of past Olympic matches and listings of past national champions.)

McManama, J., and Shondell, D.: Teaching volleyball fundamentals. *Journal of the American Association of Health, Physical Education, and Recreation,* Vol. 40:3, 1969. (An excellent article dealing with the methods used to teach the fundamentals of the game.)

Shay, C. (consultant): *Volleyball Skill Tests Manual*. American Association for Health, Physical Education and Recreation, Washington, D.C., 1969. (A manual presenting general instructions and percentiles for volleyball skills tests.)

Official Volleyball Guide. United States Volleyball Association, 1750 E. Boulder Ave., Colorado Springs, Colorado 80909.